RESCUI

FROM T

CHRIST

RESCUING SEX FROM THE CHRISTIANS

CLAYTON SULLIVAN

continuum

NEW YORK • LONDON

The Continuum International Publishing Group, 80 Maiden Lane, New York, NY 10038

The Continuum International Publishing Group Ltd., The Tower Building, 11 York Road, London SE1 7NX

Cover art: Collection: PhotoAlto; Photographer: Dominique Douieb

Cover design: Corey Kent

Library of Congress Cataloging-in-Publication Data

Sullivan, Clayton, 1930–
    Rescuing sex from the Christians / Clayton Sullivan.
      p. cm.
    Includes bibliographical references and index.
    ISBN 0-8264-1792-2 (pbk.)
    1. Sex—Religious aspects—Christianity. 2. Sexual ethics. 3. Christian ethics. 4. Consequentialism (Ethics) I. Title.
BT708.S87   2006
241'.66—dc22

                                2005031775

Printed in the United States of America

06 07 08 09 10 11   10 9 8 7 6 5 4 3 2 1

To Charlotte McDonnell

CONTENTS

PREFACE

Rescuing Sex from the Christians has not been written for the clergy. Instead, this book has been written for ordinary lay Christians (church members who sit in pews) who are psychologically tormented by what authoritative spokesmen for Christianity proclaim concerning human sexuality. Listening over the years to bishops and fundamentalist preachers, I have become increasingly vexed and perplexed over the church's disapproving attitude toward sex. Unfortunately, this negative attitude goes all the way back to the emergence of Christianity some two thousand years ago. I regret that in the Revelation to John, the last book in the New Testament, Christians who have "made it to heaven" are described as those who have not defiled themselves with women and have remained virgins (Rev 14:4). This book, contrarily, is premised on the view that our sexual longings are implanted within us by God. Our sexual longings, instead of being evil and sources of shame, are as morally neutral as our longing for food when we are hungry or our longing for sleep when we are tired. Thus, I hope this book will help readers to accept gratefully their sexuality.

In writing this book I am indebted to others. I am grateful to Henry Carrigan, editor of Continuum, and to Dr. Vivien Carver, Dr. Bonita Reinert, Dr. Paula Smithka, and Dr. Betty Drake for editorial assistance. I am also grateful to Karolyn Thompson for library research, Russlyn Castle for proofreading the text, and Beverly J. Davis, computer specialist par excellence. She has patiently typed and retyped the text of this book as it has undergone numerous revisions.

TWO
MAJOR
MISTAKES

T aking the long view, for two thousand years Christianity has maintained a disapproving attitude toward human sexuality ("sex is dirty"). As David Carr of New York's Union Theological Seminary observed, "From the outset, Christianity has depicted sex as a dangerous, chaotic, antispiritual force."[1] This negative attitude broaches the question: Why has the church over the centuries exhibited a hostile attitude toward sex? In part I of this book I shall attempt to answer that question. I shall contend that early theologians made two major mistakes in what they thought about sexuality. Their first mistake involves the story of Adam and Eve in the garden of Eden. This story is found in the second and third chapters of Genesis, the first book in the Bible. Early Christian thinkers interpreted this Genesis story factually, or historically. They believed that thousands of years ago a garden of Eden literally existed on earth and that Adam and Eve ("mankind's first couple") lived in this garden as people of flesh and blood. Early theologians failed to understand that the story about Adam and Eve is not "flesh and blood history" but instead is myth. Moreover, they read into the story ideas that are not there. The second major mistake theologians made involves what can be called the concept of the divided self— the view that every person is composed of two different parts: body and soul. The body is material; the soul is nonmaterial. These two parts, so the concept contends, are conflicted: "The soul and the body—which is inferior to the soul—are constantly at war with one another." Since human sexuality involves the body (which is inherently bad), early theologians concluded that sex must ipso facto be bad.

The discussion that immediately follows, I admit, is not an easy read. And I fear some readers will deem as tedious and abstruse my discussion of the garden of Eden and the divided self. This judgment I regret, but I believe a consideration of Adam and Eve in the garden of Eden and a consideration of the divided self are necessary if we are going to understand why the Christian religion traditionally has had a jaundiced view of human sexuality. After I have analyzed the Eden mistake and the divided self mistake, we will then be in a better position (in part II) to deal with the specific issues of masturbation, homosexuality, fornication, adultery, and prostitution. I shall deal first of all with the mistake concerning Adam and Eve in the garden of Eden.

NOTES

1. David M. Carr, *The Erotic Word* (New York: Oxford Press, 2003), 5.

CHAPTER 1

The First Mistake: Misunderstanding Adam and Eve in the Garden of Eden

Adam and Eve and the Euhemerous Fallacy

The Adam and Eve story, familiar to many westerners, can be summarized as follows: At creation's beginning God planted the garden of Eden and placed Adam and Eve (in popular thought viewed as the first man and woman on earth) in this garden. In the middle of the garden were two mysterious trees. One was the tree of life and the other was the tree of the knowledge of good and evil. Adam was commanded by God not to eat the fruit of this tree. "You may eat freely of every tree in the garden but of the tree of the knowledge of good and evil you shall not eat, for in the day you eat of it you shall die" (Gen 2:16–17). This command was disobeyed by Adam and Eve. A serpent enticed Eve to eat fruit from the tree of the knowledge of good and evil. She in turn persuaded Adam to eat the same fruit. After eating forbidden fruit, the eyes of Adam and Eve were "opened and they knew that they were naked; and they sewed fig leaves together and made loincloths for themselves" (Gen 3:7).

God disapproved of Adam and Eve's act of disobedience and decided to punish them. As punishment the woman's parturition pangs were increased. God said to Eve, "I will greatly increase your pangs in child-bearing; in pain you shall bring forth children, yet your desire shall be for your husband, and he shall rule over you" (Gen 3:16). Adam's punishment involved a cursing of the ground combined with a life's fate of wearisome labor. "Because you have listened to the voice of your wife, and have eaten of the tree about which I commanded you . . . cursed is the ground because of you; in toil you shall eat of it all the days of your life; thorns and thistles it shall bring forth for you . . . by the sweat of your face you shall eat bread until you return to the ground" (Gen 3:17–19). As a final blow Adam and Eve were expelled from the garden of Eden lest they eat of the tree of life and become immortal.

Contemporary Old Testament scholarship does not view the Adam and Eve story in Genesis as factual history. Instead, scholars today view the story as epic or myth. This story is to Judaism what the story of Pandora and her box is to Greek mythology: an attempt to explain *how* and *why* and *when* evil entered human experience. In Greek mythology Pandora was the first woman on earth. Zeus, the king of the gods, was furious because Prometheus had stolen fire from the gods and given it to men. Zeus therefore ordered Hephaestus, the god of fire, to create an evil creature whom all men would desire. In response to this command Hephaestus created a woman out of earth and water. All the gods gave her gifts (such as beauty, cunning, and knowledge of the arts). Consequently, this newly created woman was named Pandora, which literally means "all-gift." Pandora, so the legend continues, was given a box the gods commanded her not to open. Unable to resist her curiosity, she raised the box's lid and a swarm of vices, sins, diseases, and troubles escaped. Only hope was left inside the box.

Parallels between Eve and Pandora are obvious. Both were the "first woman" on earth. Both were given a negative command: "Do not open the box"; "do not eat fruit from the tree of the knowledge of good and evil." Both yielded to temptation and as a result evil descended upon mankind.

The recognition that the Adam and Eve story is myth—a Jewish parallel to the story about Pandora's box—did not become prominent in Old Testament studies until the last part of the nineteenth century, a century that witnessed a series of spectacular archaeological discoveries. One of these spectacular discoveries was the recovery of the Gilgamesh Epic. Researchers discovered this epic in the ruins of Nineveh, the capital of the old Assyrian empire that had collapsed in the seventh century B.C.E. Written in cuneiform on clay tablets, this epic relates the exploits of Gilgamesh, a Mesopotamian hero who lived in the city of Uruk (in present-day Iraq). Inquisitive persons interested in understanding the epic nature of the first eleven chapters of Genesis should—for their own instruction—read the Gilgamesh Epic; see the footnote for English translations that are readily available.[1] In addition to the exploits of Gilgamesh, the epic relates the experiences of Utnapishtim, a man frequently referred to as the Mesopotamian Noah. Utnapishtim related how the gods decided to destroy mankind by sending a devastating flood. Parallels between Utnapishtim's story of this flood and the Noah flood story in Genesis are multiple: in both stories a hero is warned of the impending disaster, is commanded to build a boat, and is instructed to gather on the boat his family and animals. In both flood stories mankind is destroyed, the boats come to rest on mountains when the flood is over, and sacrifices are offered to the gods. The discovery of the Gilgamesh Epic back in the nineteenth century was an eye-opener to Old Testament scholars. They came to see that traditions found in the opening chapters of Genesis (the creation stories, the account of Adam and Eve in the garden of Eden, the tower of Babel fiasco) are epics—stories told by the ancients concerning heroes and primeval events. All people in the ancient world—Egyptians, Assyrians, Babylonians, Greeks, and Romans—had myths. For the Jews who wrote the book of Genesis not to have had myths would have been as surprising as it would have been curious. A recognition of the mythic nature of the Adam and Eve story is, I emphasize, of recent vintage. For centuries theologians had viewed this story as factual history. They committed what I suggest can be called the Euhemerous fallacy. Euhemerous was a mythographer of the fourth century B.C.E. who interpreted (or misinterpreted) myths or epics as accounts of actual historical persons. Thus the Euhemerous fallacy is the mistake of viewing imaginary, mythical figures as historical persons. Capitulating to this fallacy, theologians—both past and present, both Catholic and Protestant—have thought of Adam and Eve as actual people of flesh and blood who lived at creation's beginning in a physical garden of Eden located in what Greek and Roman writers once referred to as Mesopotamia (again, present-day Iraq).

Parenthetically, contemporary theologians who continue to believe in a physical-literal garden of Eden fail to grapple with the question: Why hasn't the garden of Eden been located? No suggestion exists in the biblical tradition that this garden was destroyed at some point in the past. Because the Tigris and the Euphrates rivers flowed out of the garden, we know that it was located in Iraq. Surely—if the garden of Eden physically exists—modern techniques of reconnaissance (for example, air photography) would by now have discovered its precise location. Conservative theologians blissfully ignore the puzzle of why present-day researchers (biblical scholars, Near Eastern specialists, Iraqi government officials, geographers, cartographers) have not located the garden of Eden in Iraq, a small, mostly desert country the size of California. A literal garden of Eden should be easy for researchers to recognize. According to Gen 3:24, at its entrance are numerous cherubim—huge, winged, sphinxlike figures with human heads and composite bodies (part lion and part bull). Also at the entrance is a flaming sword flashing back and forth (Gen 3:24).

Furthermore, these theologians reason as follows: Originally Adam and Eve lived in the garden of Eden in a beautiful state of holiness. After eating forbidden fruit, however, they were deprived of this holiness because they had disobeyed God. By so doing they committed what theologians call original sin. This disobedient act of Adam and Eve has had tragic consequences for mankind. The human race has *fallen* (thus the expression "the fall of mankind"). Human nature has become tainted with an inclination toward moral evil. This inclination is referred to by the cumbersome term concupiscence. Moreover, the stigma of the original sin of Adam and Eve has been transmitted to their descendants. And how does this transmission of original sin take place? The answer: *through sexual intercourse. Semen is the vehicle by which the curse and stigma of original sin is passed on from one generation to the next.*

I am not contending for one moment that the line of reasoning found in the preceding paragraph ("blame our troubles on Adam and Eve because they ate forbidden fruit in the garden of Eden") makes sense to modern man. But across the centuries theologians have so reasoned. One of the early church fathers to reason this way was Augustine. He demands our attention.

Augustine of Hippo

Augustine of Hippo (not to be confused with Augustine of Canterbury) is a dominant figure in Christian theology. Because of his importance I shall digress to make one or two remarks about who he was. Augustine was born in 354 in Thagaste, a town located in what is now Algeria but which then was a part of the Roman province of Africa. His father, a pagan, was named Patricius, and his mother, a devout Christian, was named Monica. As a young man Augustine went to Carthage to study rhetoric. While a student in Carthage he lived a morally corrupt life. He took a concubine (her name is unknown) and in the year 371 she gave birth to Augustine's son, Adeodatus. Augustine, accompanied by his concubine and son, moved to Milan. There he fell under the influence of Ambrose, the city's bishop. On Easter Sunday in the year 387, Augustine was baptized by Ambrose. He eventually returned to Thagaste and from there moved to the seaport of Hippo, where he became the city's bishop. Augustine died in 430, while Hippo was being besieged by the Vandals.

Over the years Augustine was a prolific writer of letters, essays, and books. By far his two most famous works are the *Confessions*, which is autobiographical in nature, and the *City of God*, a voluminous theological treatise.

Augustine's religious beliefs expressed in the *City of God* depend largely upon his literal understanding of the Adam and Eve story, and it is fair to say he has done as much as any theologian to make this story central in Christian theology. In a word, parties as different as Billy Graham and the Roman Catholic Church have appropriated hook, line, and sinker Augustine's reasoning.

That reasoning is presented in the *City of God* as follows: When God placed Adam and Eve in paradise (Augustine's term for the garden of Eden), their life was idyllic.

> The love of the pair for God and for one another was undisturbed, and they lived in a faithful and sincere fellowship which brought great gladness to them, for what they loved was always at hand for their enjoyment. There was a tranquil avoidance of sin; and, as long as this continued, no evil of any kind intruded, from any source, to bring them sadness.[2]

Adam lived without any want for food or drink and had it within his power to live forever by eating from the tree of life (lest age decay him).[3]

> There was no corruption in the body, or arising from the body, to bring any distress to any of his senses. There was no fear of disease from within or injury from without. He enjoyed supreme health of body, and entire tranquility of soul. . . . There was nothing of sadness; neither was there any empty pleasure. Rather, true joy poured forth continually from God. . . . In his leisure, man did not know the weariness of fatigue, and sleep never pressed upon him against his will. (XIV, 26)

Moreover, no unwholesome lust was associated with the sexual organs of Adam and Eve (XIV, 26). Additionally, so Augustine believed, had Adam remained subject to his Creator, he would have passed over into the company of the angels and would have obtained, without suffering death, a blessed immortality without end (XII, 22).

But Adam was created with free will—the power of choice. He chose to rebel against God, a rebellion that would have dire consequences: "If he offended the Lord his God by using his free will proudly and disobediently, he should live, as the beasts do, subject to death: the slave of his own lust, destined to suffer eternal punishment after death" (XII, 22).

Like Adam, Eve possessed free will. Satan spoke to her through the serpent (a creature "slippery and moving in twisting coils") and enticed her to eat of the tree of the knowledge of good and evil (XIV, 11). She in turn enticed Adam to eat the same fruit. By so doing they disobeyed God. This disobedience was outrageous because so little had been asked of them: "The unrighteousness of disobeying the command was all the greater in proportion to the ease with which it could have been observed and upheld" (XIV, 12).

As a result of Adam and Eve's disobedience, so Augustine bemoaned, mankind was corrupted. Adam produced corrupt and condemned offspring: "God created man upright, for He is the author of natural beings, not, surely, of their defeats. Man, however, when he was willingly corrupted and justly condemned, engendered corrupt and condemned offspring" (XIII, 14).

A question emerges: How is this corrupt nature (original sin) passed on from one person to another or from one generation to the next? In answering this question Augustine gave the coup de grace to a wholesome attitude toward sexual intercourse. Augustine's answer: Original sin is transmitted from one person to another *through semen*.

> For we were all in that one man since all of us were that one man who fell into sin through the woman who was made from him before sin. We did not yet have individually created and apportioned shapes in which to live as individuals; what already existed was the seminal substance from which we were to be generated. Obviously, when this substance was debased through sin and shackled with the bond of death in just condemnation, no man could be born of man in any other condition. Thus from the abuse of free will has come the linked sequence of our disaster, by which the human race is conducted through an uninterrupted succession of miseries from that original depravity, as it were from a diseased root, all the way to the catastrophe of the second death that has no end. Only those who are freed through the grace of God are exempt from this fate. (XIII, 14)

Ponder Augustine's not-easy-to-follow line of reasoning (reasoning later adopted by Roman Catholicism with its contention that original sin is passed on through propagation): Man (Adam) produced corrupt

11

and condemned children. Although these corrupt children did not exist at first as individuals, nonetheless Adam's seminal substance (semen) or nature (*natura seminalis*) through which they were to be propagated by sexual intercourse did exist. Yet this seminal substance was debased by sin and was shackled with the bond of death. Hence Adam's descendants (being produced from debased semen) could not be born with any other fate than to experience an uninterrupted succession of miseries.

Elaine Pagels of Princeton University and the author of the provocative book entitled *Adam, Eve, and the Serpent* has expounded or paraphrased the just-quoted passage about Adam's seminal substance as follows:

> How can one imagine that millions of individuals not yet born were "in Adam" or in any sense, "were" Adam? Anticipating objections that would reduce his argument to absurdity, Augustine declares triumphantly that, although "we did not yet have individually created and apportioned forms in which to live as individuals," what did exist already was the "nature of the semen from which we were to be propagated." That semen itself, Augustine argues, already "shackled by the bond of death," transmits the damage incurred by sin. Hence, Augustine concludes, every human being ever conceived through semen already is born contaminated with sin. Through this astonishing argument, Augustine intends to prove that every human being is in bondage not only from birth but indeed from the moment of conception. And since he takes Adam as a corporate personality, Augustine applies his account of Adam's experience, disrupted by the first sin, to every one of his offspring (except, of course, to Christ, conceived, Augustine ingeniously argued, without semen).[4]

This association of copulation and semen with transmission of original sin partially explains—so Augustine believed—why shame surrounds sexual intercourse.

Theologians after Augustine mimic his thought. They reason as follows: "Since Augustine said it, it must be true. Therefore, we believe it." They fail to recognize that in his interpretation of Adam and Eve in paradise Augustine committed the Euhemerous fallacy, treating mythical figures as historical persons and confusing the language of myth with the language of fact. I think theologians would be less mesmerized by Augustine's interpretation of Adam and Eve if they were familiar with other ideas and beliefs that he expressed in the *City of God*. For example, Augustine believed that after the Genesis flood animals from Noah's ark were carried by angels to remote islands (XVI, 7). He accepted the possibility of monstrous races of men with only one eye in the middle of their foreheads, with feet pointing backward, and with right male breasts and left female breasts. He accepted the possibility of races of men without necks who have eyes in their shoulders and dog heads. He also accepted the possibility of females who conceived at the age of five but did not live to be more than eight years old. All of these strange creatures were descendants of Adam (XVI, 8). Augustine also believed that Hebrew was mankind's original language and that languages such as Greek and Latin were derived from Hebrew (XVI, 11). Living in North Africa, he rejected the idea that people lived on the other side of the earth (XVI, 9) and contended that the world was less than six thousand years old (XIII, 41). The *City of God* informs the reader that mountains in Sicily have always been on fire (XXI, 4), that peacock carrion (dead flesh) does not rot (XXI, 4), that female horses (mares) in Cappadocia are impregnated by the wind (XXI, 5), that diamonds cannot be destroyed by iron or fire but can be destroyed by goat's blood (XXI, 4), and that apples raised around Sodom explode when bitten into and immediately crumble into dust and ashes (XXI, 5). These beliefs about one-eyed men and nondecaying peacock carrion would be greeted with horselaughs and skepticism by contemporary theologians. Strangely enough, these same theologians are gullible when it comes to Augustine's interpretation of Adam and Eve and their expulsion from paradise. And so Augustine—with his Adam and Eve theology—has cast a dark shadow across more than a thousand years of church history. His theology is as alive today as it was back in the fifth century when he lived in North Africa in the village of Hippo.

Billy Graham and the Adam and Eve Story

Augustine's interpretation of Adam and Eve continues to live, for example, in the theology of Billy Graham, this country's evangelist par excellence. In 1991, William Martin, a sociology professor at Rice University and the holder of two degrees in religion from Harvard University, published a scholarly biography of Billy Graham entitled *A Prophet with Honor: The Billy Graham Story*. Chapter 10 is entitled "Trust and Obey" and is an exploration of Billy Graham's theology. Martin begins the chapter with these words:

> Billy Graham's theology was anything but abstruse. The heart of his preaching was and would ever remain a short list of straightforward affirmations. A sovereign God has revealed his will to humans in the Bible, his inspired, accurate, and fully dependable Word. Humans are sinful and corrupt, but if they accept God's offer of grace, made possible by the redeeming work of the crucified, risen, and living Christ, their sinful nature can be supernaturally transformed—"born again"—and after death they will live forever in heaven. Without question, the simplicity of this scheme helps account for the widespread and enduring popularity of Evangelical Christianity.[5]

Later in this same chapter Martin writes:

> The cornerstone of Graham's theology, of course, was his unshakable belief that the Bible is God's actual Word. His literalism required him . . . to believe that Adam and Eve were actual historical beings, "created full-grown with every mental and physical faculty developed." . . . Adam, in the Orthodox Evangelical view, was created sinless but equipped with free will. Because he used that freedom to disobey God and ate of the tree of the knowledge of good and evil, he fell into a state of sinful, guilt-ridden rebellion against God, a state passed along to all of his descendants. Left to their own devices, humans will live a miserable, unsatisfying life and spend eternity separated from God.[6]

A perusal of Graham's books and sermons reveals that Martin's analysis is on target. In 1965, Graham published a book entitled *World Aflame*. Chapter 7 is entitled "Man's Fatal Disease." In this chapter Graham asserts: "When we come to the entrance of sin into the human race, the Bible is much more specific. It teaches that, through one act of one man, sin came into the world, and with it all the universal consequences of sin. This one man was Adam, and this one act was the partaking of the fruit of the tree of the knowledge of good and evil that God had forbidden."[7]

Additional Graham quotations would be superfluous. Suffice it to say: Billy Graham's Augustinian interpretation of Adam as a person of flesh and blood has been held by multiple theologians, including many who came before him. John Wesley, Methodism's founder, also held a historical view of Adam and the fall of man.[8] So did Martin Luther, the father of the Protestant Reformation.[9] So did John Calvin, a French theologian and a major church reformer of the sixteenth century. Calvin wrote what is considered by many to be the authoritative, systematic theology of the Protestant Reformation. It is entitled *Institutes of the Christian Religion*. A reading of book II of the *Institutes* reveals that Calvin reasoned like Billy Graham and Augustine when it comes to Adam and the havoc he has brought upon mankind. A typical quotation from the *Institutes* is as follows:

> There is nothing absurd, then, in supposing that, when Adam was despoiled, human nature was left naked and destitute, or that when he was infected with sin, contagion crept into human nature. Hence, rotten branches came forth from a rotten root, which transmitted their rottenness to the other twigs sprouting from them. . . . That is, the beginning of corruption in Adam was such that it was conveyed in a perpetual stream from the ancestors into their descendants.[10]

Roman Catholicism and the Adam and Eve Story

This blame of mankind's corruption on Adam and Eve is also the warp and woof of theology in the Roman Catholic Church—Christendom's largest church, with more than a billion members.[11] In 1994, the Roman Catholic Church produced a summary of its beliefs entitled *Catechism of the Catholic Church*.[12] The late Pope John Paul II wrote the book's introduction. In his introduction he observed that the catechism had required six years to write and was officially approved by him (on June 25, 1992) as a "statement of the Church's faith and Catholic doctrine" (5). Additionally, John Paul observed that the new catechism was offered to every person "who wants to know what the Catholic Church believes" (6). In Augustinian fashion, the catechism blames mankind's sinfulness on the behavior of "our first parents" in the garden of Eden. Ponder these quotations taken verbatim from the catechism:

> The account of the fall in Genesis 3 . . . affirms a primeval event, a deed that took place *at the beginning of the history of man*. Revelation gives us the certainty of faith that the whole of human history is marked by the original fault freely committed by our first parents. (100–101, paragraphs 399 and 400) [13]
>
> Scripture portrays the tragic consequences of this first disobedience. Adam and Eve immediately lose the grace of original holiness. . . . The harmony in which they had found themselves, thanks to original justice, is now destroyed: The control of the soul's spiritual faculties over the body is shattered; the union of man and woman becomes subject to tensions, their relations henceforth marked by lust and domination. (102, paragraph 403)
>
> Following St. Paul, the Church has always taught that the overwhelming misery which oppresses men and their inclination toward evil and death cannot be understood apart from their connection with Adam's sin and the fact that he has transmitted to us a sin with which we are all born afflicted, a sin which is the "death of the soul." (102, paragraph 404)
>
> How did the sin of Adam become the sin of all his descendants? . . . By yielding to the tempter, Adam and Eve committed a *personal sin*, but this sin affected *the human nature* that they would then transmit *in a fallen state*. It is a sin which will be transmitted by propagation to all mankind, that is, by the transmission of a human nature deprived of original holiness and justice. (102, paragraph 405)
>
> As a result of original sin, human nature is weakened in its powers; subject to ignorance, suffering, and the domination of death; and inclined to sin {this inclination is called concupiscence}. (105, paragraph 419)

We therefore hold, with the Council of Trent, that original sin is transmitted with human nature "by propagation." (105)[14]

The preceding quotations, I emphasize, are taken from the recently published *Catechism of the Catholic Church*. Two of these quotations contain the word "propagation." *This term is an oblique reference to sexual intercourse leading to pregnancy.* To propagate means for a man and woman to engage in coitus, which then results in the woman becoming pregnant. Thus the catechism teaches that "fallen" human nature (deprived of original holiness and justice) is passed on from one generation to another through propagation, that is, through sexual intercourse. This conception of sexual intercourse as the vehicle by which original sin is transmitted from one person to another explains why some Catholic thinkers have a negative attitude toward sexual intercourse. Because of its transmitting association with original sin, sexual intercourse—in their minds—is a "nasty" deed. In 1930, John McHugh and Charles Callan, Dominican scholars, published a two-volume work entitled *Moral Theology*. With reference to sexual intercourse they wrote, "Now, sex pleasure has been ordained by God as an inducement to perform an act which is both *disgusting* in itself and *burdensome* in its consequences—an act, too, which has for its purpose the propagation and education of children."[15] Furthermore, "Sexual intercourse, though lawful, occasions a feeling of shame" (503). McHugh and Callan categorize sexual intercourse with passions that are among "the lower, animal, or carnal pleasures, since they are common to man and beast, and are strongly rebellious against reason. The special virtue of temperance is necessary, then, to make men follow reason, not Bacchus or Venus" (485). Moreover, sexual pleasures should never be used in marriage "except for the procreation of children" (485).

This antipathy toward sexual intercourse (a "disgusting" act that is the "burdensome" vehicle of original sin) explains why Catholic theologians place a premium on Jesus' virgin birth (more properly, his virginal conception). Not having a human father combined with Mary's immaculate conception protected Jesus from the stain of original sin.[16]

A Marinade of Sin and Shame

This chapter began with the observation that for two thousand years the Christian religion has maintained a disapproving attitude toward human sexuality. Why has this been the case? The way theologians from Augustine to Billy Graham to the late Pope John Paul II have treated the Adam and Eve story provides a partial answer. They have used the Adam and Eve myth to advance the view that sexual intercourse is the means by which the virus of original sin (embedded in semen) is passed on from one generation to the next. Christians who possess this negative understanding of sexual intercourse find it diffi-cult—if not impossible—to have a positive attitude toward human sex-uality. Thus Christian thinkers have steeped human sexuality in a marinade of sin and shame, and have unloaded upon millions of gullible believers feelings of guilt about their sexuality. Better to be celibate, they believe, than to engage in "disgusting" sexual intercourse!

Also contributing to this negativity about sex, however, is the under-standing theologians have had about persons as divided selves. I shall now deal briefly with this issue.

NOTES

1. Translations of the Gilgamesh Epic are available in the Penguin Classics Series: N. K. Sandars, *The Epic of Gilgamesh* (New York: Penguin Books, 1972); Andrew George, *The Epic of Gilgamesh: A New Translation* (New York: Penguin Books, 2000).

2. Augustine, *City of God*, XIV, 10. Quotations from *City of God* are taken mainly from R. W. Dyson, *The City of God against the Pagans* (New York: Cam-bridge University Press, 2001). To exaggerate Augustine's influence on Christ-ian theology is a practical impossibility. As confirmation of this statement I quote the late Willistone Walker, a church historian of Yale University. In his classic *A History of the Christian Church* ([New York: Charles Scribner's Sons, 1970], 160), Walker wrote as follows:

> In Augustine the ancient church reached its highest religious attainment
> since apostolic times. Though his influence in the East was to be rela-

tively slight, owing to the nature of the questions with which he was primarily concerned, all Western Christianity was to become his debtor. Such superiority as Western religious life came to possess over that of the East was primarily his bequest to it. He was to be the father of much that was most characteristic in medieval Roman Catholicism. He was to be the spiritual ancestor, no less, of much in the Reformation. . . .

3. *City of God*, XIV, 26.

4. Elaine Pagels, *Adam, Eve, and the Serpent* (New York: Random House, 1988), 109. The scientific thought of Aristotle is possibly hovering in the background of Augustine's assertions about semen. Contemporary readers find it difficult to see a connection between what people become and the semen from which they "were to be propagated." But consider Aristotle's work entitled *Generation of Animals*. In this treatise he devoted page after page to a discussion of semen. He posed the question: "Has the semen soul, or not?" Aristotle's answer: "It is plain therefore that semen both has soul, and is soul, potentially." Augustine—following Aristotle—could reason like this: since semen is soul and has soul, it follows that damaged semen (corrupted by Adam's disobedience) will produce damaged souls. For the Aristotle quote just cited see *The Complete Works of Aristotle* (Princeton, N.J.: Princeton University Press, 1984), 1: 1141.

5. William Martin, *A Prophet with Honor: The Billy Graham Story* (New York: William Morrow & Company, Inc., 1991), 155.

6. Ibid., 156–57.

7. Billy Graham, *World Aflame* (Garden City, N.Y.: Doubleday, 1965), 67.

8. John Wesley, *Explanatory Notes upon the New Testament* (New York: Eaton & Mains, 1754), 375.

9. Martin Luther, *Luther's Works: Lectures on Genesis* (Saint Louis: Concordia Publishing House, 1958), I:101–36.

10. John Calvin, *Institutes of the Christian Religion* (Philadelphia: Westminster Press, 1977), I:250.

11. *The World Almanac and Book of Facts* (New York: World Almanac Books, 2005), 734.

12. *Catechism of the Catholic Church* (Liguori, Mo.: Liguori Publications, 1994), 5.

13. Parenthetically, Catholic theologians are forbidden by the *Humani generis* of Pope Pius XII of positing the existence of people not physically descended from Adam and Eve. They must maintain that the entire human race is descended from Adam and Eve because any other view would conflict with the church's teaching on original sin.

14. The Council of Trent also decreed: "If one should not acknowledge that the first man Adam, on transgressing God's command in paradise, did not immediately lose the holiness and justice in which he had been constituted . . . let him be anathema" (Pope John Paul II, *The Theology of the Body* [Boston: Pauline Books & Media, 1997], 99).

15. John McHugh and Charles Callan, *Moral Theology* (New York: Joseph F. Wagner, Inc., 1930), II:508. Italics added.

16. The immaculate conception dogma is misunderstood by non-Catholics. It is a dogma "of the Roman Catholic Church stating that the Blessed Virgin Mary was preserved free from original sin from the first instance of her coming into life. This doctrine should not be confused with the teaching concerning the Virgin Birth of Christ by Mary. . . . Nor does the Immaculate Conception connote any virginal birth of Mary herself or any extraordinary occurrences connected with the action of her own parents in giving her life. Mary was conceived and born in the normal human way" (Charles E. Sheedy, "Immaculate Conception," *Encyclopedia Americana* [Danbury, Conn.: Grolier, 1999], 14:801–802.

Some Roman Catholics also have difficulty understanding what is meant by the immaculate conception. Tim Russert of *Meet the Press* fame has written a book entitled *Big Russ and Me*, in which he tells about attending Canisius High School, a Jesuit institution in Buffalo, New York. With reference to Canisius, Tim Russert wrote:

"One of the first things I learned at Canisius was that contrary to what most of us believed, the Immaculate Conception is not the same as the virgin birth, and that it refers not to the birth of Jesus, but to the birth of Mary. In order to be pure enough to become the mother of Jesus, Mary was conceived free from original sin. Over the years, I've made hundreds of dollars by betting my fellow Catholics in Buffalo, in Washington, and even in Rome that they couldn't tell me the real meaning of the Immaculate Conception" (Tim Russert, *Big Russ and Me* [New York: Miramax Books, 2004], 163).

CHAPTER 2

The Second Mistake: The Concept of the Divided Self

I shall begin this discussion of the divided (or conflicted) self by posing several questions: How are persons put together? How many "parts" does a person have? Or is it a false move to conceive of any person as being composed of different parts? Instead, are people put together like boiled custard with everything blended together and with no distinguishable parts? Over the years such questions about human composition have received different answers. One of the oldest—and most widely accepted answers—is the view of the divided self. This view contends that every person consists basically of two very different parts: the *body*, which is material in nature, and the *soul*, which is immaterial in nature. The material body can be seen with the eyes and touched with human hands while the immaterial soul cannot be seen with the eyes or touched with human hands.

For reflective persons in the ancient world this body-soul division had moral significance. They believed that the root source of many of our moral problems is the fact that we live in bodies—physical bodies of flesh and blood that present all kinds of problems. Our bodies get sick. They can be wounded and as a result experience pain. They must constantly be provided with food, drink, clothing, and shelter. They require rest and sleep. Our bodies age and as we age our bodies grow feeble (justifying the quip that "growing old is not for sissies"). Moreover, our bodies, so the ancients believed, seem to have a mind or will of their own. They are permeated with drives and passions that overwhelm or vex our souls. This conflict between body and soul is what I mean by the concept of the divided self—the view that our bodies and souls are conflicted, that they are frequently at war with each other. Or if not at war, at least they are unfriendly to one another. In the discussion that follows I will show how this view has dominated philosophical-religious thought for centuries. Time and again the body (with its needs and impulses) has been viewed as inferior to and as rebellious toward the soul. What does this conflict between body and soul have to do with human sexuality? Christian interpreters have reasoned as follows: Since male and female sexual organs are parts of the body and are dominated by lust, they are ipso facto objects of shame. Moreover, by emphasizing the divided self and shame concerning genitalia (sexual organs made of flesh), Christian moralists have caused credulous Christians to feel guilty about their sexual desires. On the pages that follow I shall contend, contrariwise, that sexual desires are natural—as natural as desires for food and drink—and should be viewed as wholesome, not evil.

Socrates and the Divided Self

I begin our examination of the concept of the divided self by heeding briefly the life and thought of an old-timer by the name of Socrates, a Greek philosopher. This is a logical starting place because early Greek thinkers such as Socrates were committed to the concept, which is sometimes referred to as Hellenistic dualism. Socrates was born in Athens in 469 B.C.E. At that time Athens—thanks to a ruler named Pericles—was an impressive city. The Parthenon, an architectural marvel, had been erected on the Acropolis. Athenians had built a navy and had established colonies overseas. The city's army had defeated Persian invaders led by Darius and Xerxes. Thus Socrates was born into a city experiencing a golden age.

Married to a shrew named Xanthippe, Socrates can be aptly described as Athens's oddball or maverick par excellence. He had bulging eyes, a bald head, flat nostrils, and a bushy beard. He wore ragged clothes and walked around the streets of Athens with bare feet. Not a wealthy person, Socrates was a stonemason by trade. For a time he was a foot soldier (a hoplite) in the Athenian army. He curiously believed he heard a "voice" that guided him in his words and conduct. He delighted in questioning fellow Athenians about their beliefs (frequently proving their beliefs to be wrong). From a historical viewpoint he is remembered as the philosopher who changed the direction of philosophy from natural science to ethics.

Socrates' life, unfortunately, ended on a tragic note. Athens and Sparta became involved in what historians refer to as the Peloponnesian War. While the war was being waged, several of Socrates' admirers betrayed Athens by going over to the side of Sparta and Socrates was blamed for their treachery. In the emotional backlash after the war the Athenians put Socrates on trial on charges of impiety and corrupting the youth of Athens. He was tried before a jury, found guilty, and sentenced to death by drinking hemlock. In the hours before his execution Socrates engaged in conversation with several friends. This conversation was later reconstructed by Plato, an admirer of Socrates, in a document known as the *Phaedo*. In this conversation Socrates and his friends discussed a number of issues, one of which was the desirability or undesirability of death. While discussing this topic Socrates revealed that he believed in the divided self. He believed a distinction should be made between the body and the soul. Moreover, he had a positive attitude toward the soul and a negative attitude toward the body. Consider these words of Socrates from the *Phaedo*:

> Have we not found a path of thought which seems to bring us and our argument to the conclusion, that while we are in the body, and while the soul is infected with the evils of the body, our desire will not be satisfied and our desire is of the truth. For the body is a source of endless trouble to us by reason of the mere requirement of food; and is liable also to diseases which overtake and impede us in the search after true

23

being: it fills us full of loves, and lusts, and fears, and fancies of all kinds, and endless foolery, and in fact, as men say, takes away from us the power of thinking at all. Whence come wars, and fightings, and factions? Whence but from the body and the lusts of the body? Wars are occasioned by the love of money, and money has to be acquired for the sake and in the service of the body; and by reason of all these impediments we have no time to give to philosophy; and, last and worst of all, even if we are at leisure and betake ourselves to some speculation, the body is always breaking in upon us, causing turmoil and confusion in our enquiries, and so amazing us that we are prevented from seeing the truth. It has been proved to us by experience that if we would have pure knowledge of anything we must be quit of the body.[1]

In this excerpt the body is described by Socrates as possessing evils, as a source of endless trouble, as disease prone, as a source of lusts, fears, and endless foolery, and as the cause of wars, turmoil, and confusion. The *Phaedo* abounds with other pro-soul and anti-body remarks. For example, the soul is in the very likeness of the divine and is immortal, intellectual, and indissoluble, while the body is the very likeness of the human, the mortal, the unintellectual, and the dissoluble (465). As far as Socrates was concerned, the body was a "prison with bars" to the soul (468). This prison metaphor is similar to his remark that the body is a tomb for the soul (190).

It is not surprising, therefore, that Socrates welcomed death. He believed that through death his soul would be released from "the chains of the body" (451). Upon death his soul would depart with no bodily taint, never voluntarily having had connection with the body (465).

In short, Socrates possessed a negative attitude toward the body and a positive attitude toward the soul. To his mind every person is composed of a part that is good (the soul) and a part that is bad (the body). Moreover, Socrates was committed to the concept of the divided self in the sense that the body and the soul are divided against each other. Their relationship is one of hostility. This body-soul antagonism was a prominent motif in ancient Greek philosophy, and this motif influenced early Christian thinkers such as Saint Paul, to whom I now turn.

Saint Paul and the Divided Self

An influential theologian of the first century, Saint Paul wrote documents—such as his letters to the Romans and to the Galatians—that became parts of the New Testament. His contributions were of such significance that he is revered to this day by the church. Like Socrates, Paul referred time and again to the body. Understandably, he used the word "body" more than once to refer to his external physique. Thus he could write: "From now on, let no one make trouble for me; for I carry the marks of Jesus branded on my body" (Gal 6:17).

But Paul also on occasion used the term "body" (the Greek word is *soma*) in the same way Socrates did: as the "part" of a person that is the source and locale of moral discord. The body is the domain of lusts. "Do not let sin exercise dominion in your mortal bodies, to make you obey their passions" (Rom 6:12). "We know that our old self was crucified with him so that the body of sin [that is, a body that belongs to sin] might be destroyed, and we might no longer be enslaved to sin" (Rom 6:6). Because of the body's harmful role in his life, Paul felt it was necessary for him to punish and to enslave his body (1 Cor 9:27).

A study of Paul's letters reveals, however, that instead of the word "body" he preferred the word "flesh" (admittedly, from a psychological viewpoint, a crude term) as the locale of harmful impulses and as a source of vices. The Greek word Paul used for flesh is *sarx*, which has the basic meaning of the flesh material (the soft part of bodies composed chiefly of muscle) common to people and to animals. *Sarx* bears this purely physiological meaning in Paul's observation that "not all flesh is alike, but there is one flesh for human beings, another for animals, another for birds, and another for fish" (1 Cor 15:39). Similarly, the term bears this physiological meaning when Paul refers to his thorn in the flesh (2 Cor 12:7).

But (and here we encounter the concept of the divided self) Paul also used "flesh" (*sarx*) in an ethical sense: not merely as the stuff out of which bodies are made, but as the basis—the "launching pad"—from which sin attacks people. To Paul's mind our flesh is not inert or neutral. Rather it is problematic and alive with unwholesome desires and impulses. With this meaning in mind Paul wrote to the Galatian Christians as follows:

> Live by the Spirit, I say, and do not gratify the desires of the flesh. For what the flesh desires is opposed to the Spirit, and what the Spirit desires is opposed to the flesh. . . . Now the works of the flesh are obvious: fornication, impurity, licentiousness, idolatry, sorcery, enmities, strife, jealousy, anger, quarrels, dissensions, factions, envy, drunkenness, carousing, and things like these. I am warning you, as I warned you before: those who do such things will not inherit the kingdom of God. (Gal 5:16–21)

He continues by comparing the Spirit with the flesh: "By contrast, the fruit of the Spirit is love, joy, peace, patience, kindness, generosity, faithfulness, gentleness, and self-control. There is no law against such things. And those who belong to Christ Jesus have *crucified the flesh* with its passions and desires. If we live by the Spirit, let us also be guided by the Spirit" (Gal 5:22–25, my emphasis).

Thus for Paul people confront a choice. They can either decide to live by the flesh or they can decide to live by the Spirit (a term I find fuzzy). To convey this choice he employed an illustration from agriculture—the sowing of seed. "Do not be deceived; God is not mocked, for you reap whatever you sow. If you sow to your own flesh, you will reap corruption from the flesh; but if you sow to the Spirit, you will reap eternal life from the Spirit. So let us not grow weary in doing what is right, for we will reap at harvest time, if we do not give up" (Gal 6:7–9).

I am emphasizing the insight that for Paul our flesh (there is no evidence he used the term symbolically) is a Pandora's box of vices (everything from envy to fornication) and of malignant impulses. It has unsavory desires and produces a harvest of corruption. Consequently—so Paul believed—it should be crucified. This negative view of flesh and body is a cornerstone belief of the concept of the divided self. The flesh belongs to one's "lower" or "animal" nature and is in conflict with and is a hindrance to a higher way of life (which Paul describes as living by the "Spirit" or by the "Spirit of Christ" or by the "Spirit of God"). This contrast between Spirit life and flesh life becomes evident when we ponder Paul's advice to the Roman Christians: "So then, brothers and sisters, we are debtors, not to the flesh, to live according to the flesh— for if you live according to the flesh, you will die; but if by the Spirit you put to death the deeds of the body, you will live" (Rom 8:12–13).

Paul's thoughts on flesh and body easily lead to the following line of reasoning: once a person believes his flesh and body are sources of vices, and believes vices such as fornication are sexual in nature, and acknowledges that genitalia are involved in fornication, it is easy for that person to commit the fallacy of division (the fallacy of attributing characteristics of a whole to its parts) and conclude that *all* sexual activities involving the genitalia are sinful—or if not sinful, at least embarrassing or shameful. At this point we must bear in mind that there is no document in the New Testament comparable to the Song of Solomon in the Old Testament. The Song of Solomon, a secular love poem portraying erotic love between two young people who are not yet betrothed, rejoices in the loving pleasures of the body, an attitude not seen in the New Testament.

Augustine and the Divided Self

Over the years theologians intensified Paul's negative attitude toward flesh and body. The shame regarding genital organs (the penis and pubic areas) became a favored point for intensification. Theologians did this by elaborating even further the Adam and Eve story in the book of Genesis. Consider, for example, what Augustine conjectured in *City of God*. According to Augustine, divine grace forsook Adam and Eve immediately after they had eaten of the tree of the knowledge of good and evil. Moreover, they became "appalled at the nakedness of their own bodies. Thus, they took fig leaves, which were perhaps the first things to come to hand in their confusion of mind, and covered their shameful parts with them. For though their members remained the same as they were at first, they had not originally been a source of shame to them."[2] Ponder Augustine's just-cited opinion that genitalia (the penis and vagina) are "shameful parts" and a "source of shame."

But Augustine was not content merely to heap disgrace on genitalia. Instead, he also intensified Paul's view—expressed in Gal 5:17—that the flesh (behaving autonomously) possesses its own desires and is opposed to the Spirit. In other words, Augustine postulated an extravagant flesh-body rebellion. For him the flesh or body is a rogue unto itself, a lustful rebel against the soul, the source of spontaneous sexual desire.

This flesh-body rebellion can be seen in Augustine's observation that Adam and Eve—after their act of disobedience—became aware of

> a new stirring of their flesh, which had become disobedient to them as a punishment, in requital of their own disobedience to God. For the soul, now taking delight in its own freedom to do wickedness, and disdaining to serve God, was itself deprived of the erstwhile subjection of the body to it. Because it had of its own free will forsaken its superior Lord, it no longer held its own inferior servant in obedience to its will. Nor could it in any way keep the flesh in subjection, as it would always have been able to do if it had itself remained subject to God. Then began the flesh to lust against the Spirit, from which we are born. (XIII, 13)

Commenting further on the intractability of the body, Augustine observed that on occasion lust (libido) "arises unwanted; sometimes, on the other hand, it forsakes the eager lover, and desire grows cold in the body even while burning in the mind. Thus strangely, then, does lust refuse to serve not only the desire to beget, but even the lust for lewd enjoyment" (XIV, 16).

Thus Augustine (presupposing the concept of the divided self) asserted that as a result of Adam's sin the soul lost control of the body (particularly its genital organs). In *City of God*'s book 14, chapter 24, Augustine gave examples of how people can control various parts of their bodies. Some people can move their ears, either singly or both at once. Others can move the hair on their scalp and imitate the sounds of birds and beasts. Some, so Augustine curiously claims, can produce music by expelling body gas through their anus. Furthermore, they expel this gas without producing odor. But alas! Genital organs—when excited by lust—cannot be controlled by the soul. To Augustine's mind this loss of control (caused by lust) combined with spontaneous sexual desire is proof of the effect of original sin on the descendants of Adam and Eve. Thus Augustine wrote:

> It is right, therefore, to be greatly ashamed of this lust, and it is right that the members which it moves or fails to move by its own right, so to speak, and not completely in accord with our will, should be called shameful, which they were not called before man's sin. For, as it is written, "And they were naked, and were not ashamed." This was not because they did not know that they were naked; rather, their nakedness was not yet disgraceful, because lust did not yet arouse those members independently of their will. The flesh did not yet give testimony, as it were, of man's disobedience by disobedience of its own. (XIV, 17)

This last statement concerning the testimony of the flesh is significant: the flesh—by a disobedience of its own—provides testimony of man's disobedience to God. Disobedient and uncontrollable sexual desire or lust (rooted in the flesh) was—I repeat—for Augustine irrefutable evidence of original sin. This explains why he wrote:

> Without any doubt, then, human nature is ashamed of its lust, and deservedly ashamed. For the disobedient nature of this lust, which has entirely subdued the organs of generation to its own urges and snatched them from the power of the will, is enough to show what retribution has been visited upon man for that first disobedience. And it was fitting that this retribution should appear especially in that part of the body which brings about the generation of the very nature that was changed for the worse through that first and great sin. That sin, perpetrated when all mankind existed in one man, brought ruin upon them all, and so no one can be rescued from the toils of that sin, which was punished by God's justice, unless the sin is expiated in each man singly by the grace of God. (XIV, 20)

I previously observed that any person who views sexual intercourse as the means by which original sin is passed on from one generation to the next will find it difficult or impossible to have a positive attitude toward human sexuality. Similarly, any person who views genitalia as "shameful parts," who views spontaneous sexual desire as evidence of

29

original sin and who believes that the body and soul are conflicted, will likewise find it difficult or impossible to have an approving attitude toward human sexuality. These views perpetuate the concept of the divided self, and they explain why scores of Christians are ashamed of and embarrassed by spontaneous, unsought sexual desires.

Parenthetically, the concept of the divided self assumed a new form in the seventeenth century in the thought of René Descartes, the father of modern philosophy. Instead of accepting the Socratic distinction between the body and the soul, Descartes posited a distinction between the mind and the body. Human beings, according to Descartes, are composed of physical bodies and immaterial minds. Pursuing this dualist theory, Descartes grappled with the questions: How can these entirely different entities intermingle with one another? How can they interact? Descartes' curious answer: They intermingle through the pineal gland in the center of the brain. Descartes should be congratulated for recognizing and confronting this intermingling puzzle. How do the body and the soul or the body and the mind interact? This puzzle eluded both Paul and Augustine.

Descartes in his own time was challenged by Benedict Spinoza, the Dutch philosopher. In our time Descartes is being challenged by neuroscientists such as Dr. Antonio Damasio of the University of Iowa, who contends that mind and body are unified.[3]

The concept of the divided self, so important to Socrates, Paul, and Augustine, is being abandoned by modern medicine and psychology. Today people are viewed as psychosomatic wholes. We no longer believe that the unruly body (or our unruly flesh)—acting autonomously—has a "mind of its own."

By Way of Recapitulation

I have contended that theologians made two major mistakes that have had a devastating impact on Christianity's attitude toward sexuality. First, they interpreted the Adam and Eve story as literal history and "read into" this story the idea that sexual intercourse is the means by which the virus of original sin is passed on (like a venereal disease) from one person to another. Second, they adopted the Socratic view that the body (inferior to the soul) is a domain of lusts of which we should be ashamed.

Even more devastating, however, for a positive attitude toward human sexuality are Jesus' "hard" sayings concerning sex, the family, and marriage. Later in this book I will give attention to Jesus' "hard" sayings concerning the latter two subjects. Assuming that the Christian religion is somehow based on what Jesus said and did, these sayings make it difficult to understand how there can be a "Christian" understanding of marriage and the family. At this point, however, I want to give attention to Jesus' lustful eye admonition, which appears in the Sermon on the Mount: "You have heard that it was said 'You shall not commit adultery.' But I say to you that everyone who looks at a woman with lust has already committed adultery with her in his heart" (Matt 5:27–28). Jesus' admonition about the lustful eye is followed by draconian advice: "If your right eye causes you to sin, tear it out and throw it away; it is better for you to lose one of your members than for your whole body to be thrown into hell" (Matt 5:29). Jesus' lustful eye remark can be restated in contemporary terms as follows: "Every man who experiences spontaneous arousal of his libido (sex drive) when looking at a woman has already committed adultery with her in his heart."

This lustful eye remark is problematic. The unsought and spontaneous stimulation of the male libido is—from a psychological viewpoint—as natural as experiencing hunger pangs after going without food or as natural as experiencing sleepiness after prolonged wakefulness. Christian interpreters strive to get around this admonition by contending that Jesus never spoke these words. Thus E. P. Sanders, a noted New Testament scholar at Duke University, suggests that the lustful eye remark—rather than being an authentic word of Jesus—instead reflects the moral perfectionism that is wrongly attributed to Jesus by the unknown author of Matthew's gospel.[4] Sanders goes on to argue that Jesus did not live "a stern and strict life" (203) and was compassionate toward human frailty (204). Moreover, "admonition to eliminate feelings that are common to humanity is not a characteristic of Jesus' teaching generally" (202).

Regardless of whether the prohibition of lustful thoughts is or is not an authentic word of Jesus, there can be no doubt that this prohibition has received attention by Christian moralists. They contend that the remark shows that Jesus believed thoughts are as blameworthy as acts. Therefore, Christians should not only avoid sinful acts but should strive for purity of thought. "The lustful eye prohibition reflects the inwardness of Jesus' moral teachings," so Christian moralists reason. The trouble or weakness with this line of reasoning is its presupposition that stimulation of the libido is immoral. It leads to the conclusion that this body instinct is sinful by its very nature, that it is a wild horse that must be tamed. This way of thinking reflects the theory of the divided self that I have just discussed.

Jesus' lustful eye judgment has been particularly emphasized by the late Pope John Paul II. In 1997, he published a book entitled *The Theology of the Body*.[5] This book can be described as a lengthy exposition of Jesus' lustful eye remark—a remark that John Paul contended was the "key to the theology of the body" (104). John Paul was so concerned about lustful eyes that he made the absurd and astonishing observation that a husband can commit adultery by looking lustfully at his wife: "Adultery in the heart is committed not only because man looks in this way at a woman who is not his wife, but *precisely* because he looks at a woman in this way. Even if he looked in this way at the woman who is his wife, he could likewise commit adultery in his heart" (157).

Paul and Augustine are two theologians who stand at the headwaters of the Christian religion. They have bequeathed to Christianity an anti-sexual legacy that lingers to this day. Or to express the matter colloquially, traditional Christianity has deliberately chosen to take a dim view of sex. Take, by way of example, the church's veneration of celibacy (the state of having no sex by having no spouse). With its commitment to the concept of the divided self and with its veneration of Saint Paul, who wished that all people were unmarried like him (1 Cor 7:7), the church over the centuries has applauded celibacy. Prior to Christianity's emergence, perpetual celibacy was practiced in neither the Gentile nor Jewish worlds (an exception was the Essene community at Qumran). To be unmarried and childless was—especially for Jews—a disgrace. But Christianity introduced a new way of viewing perpetual celibacy. The Gospel of Luke (20:35–36) suggests that the unmarried state reflects the heavenly realm where there is no marriage. Paul commended perpetual celibacy as a way of life for those who had the moral backbone to practice it. Perpetual celibacy was a foundation stone of the monastic movement that gained headway in the church in the late third century. Monks fled to the desert to live lives of isolation, prayer, and abstinence from sex. Eventually, a struggle developed within the church over the question: Should bishops, priests, and deacons also be celibate? The Eastern Orthodox Church to this day does not permit bishops to marry (although it does allow deacons and priests to marry). Gregory VII is remembered as the pope (1073–85) who imposed celibacy on priests in the Western church. Undergirding these developments is the view that celibacy is "higher" or "more noble" than marriage. In 1967, Pope Paul VI issued an encyclical entitled *Sacerdotailis Caelibatus* (The Celibacy of the Priest). This encyclical begins with the assertion: "Priestly celibacy has been guarded by the Church for centuries as a brilliant jewel and retains its value undiminished. . . ." But is celibacy a brilliant jewel? Or is it a revolt against the way we are created? Is it a capitulation to the concept of the divided self?

Celibacy is not the only illustration of the church's negative attitude toward human sexuality. This we-don't-approve-of-sex attitude has seeped into other areas. The church looks with disapproval on masturbation. The church has been savage in its condemnation of homosexuality. It disapproves of sexual intercourse between unmarried men and women and has given to such intercourse the label of fornication, a pejorative term. Likewise, the church has looked with disapproval on prostitution. Yet the church has never been forced to explain *why* activities such as masturbation, homosexuality, and prostitution are immoral or sinful. On the pages that follow I shall employ on more than one occasion the term "disapproval dilemma." By this expression I refer to the way in which the church becomes discombobulated (confronting a dilemma) when asked to explain *why* a practice such as masturbation is immoral or sinful. In other words, the church knows which sexual acts it considers to be immoral, but it has never explicated *why* those sexual acts are immoral. The morality of sexual acts needs open-minded examination.

I contend that the moment has arrived when views adopted by the church on various aspects of human sexuality need to be reexamined. Without a revision of these views Christianity—alas!—will continue to have a hostile attitude toward human sexuality. And Christians will continue to steep in a marinade of guilt and shame. In part II, which follows, I will reexamine and critique the church's attitude toward masturbation, homosexuality, fornication, adultery, and prostitution.

NOTES

1. Plato, *The Dialogues of Plato* (New York: Random House, 1937), 1: 449–50.

2. Augustine, *City of God*, XIII, 13. Quotations from *The City of God* are taken mainly from R. W. Dyson, *The City of God Against the Pagans* (New York: Cambridge University Press, 2001).

3. See, for example, an illuminating article about Dr. Antonio Damasio (Emily Eakin, "I Feel, Therefore I Am," *New York Times*, April 19, 2003, A15, 17). Damasio has advanced his views in such books as *Descartes' Error: Emotion, Reason, and the Human Brain* (New York: Putnam, 1994) and the recently published *Looking for Spinoza: Joy, Sorrow, and the Feeling Brain* (New York: Harcourt, 2003).

4. E. P. Sanders, *The Historical Figure of Jesus* (New York: Penguin Books, 1993), 201. Sanders's book is a superb presentation of post-Enlightenment research into the life of the historical Jesus.

5. John Paul II, *The Theology of the Body* (Boston: Pauline Books, 1997).

HUMAN SEXUALITY AND THE HARM PRINCIPLE

I began part I of this book with the phrase "taking the long view": "Taking the long view, for two thousand years Christianity has maintained a disapproving attitude toward human sexuality ('sex is dirty')." I want to begin part II with the same phrase. Taking the long view, the church during its two thousand-year history has intruded time and again into areas it should not have entered. A classic example of the church "throwing its weight around" in an area where it had no expertise was its intrusion into the physical sciences. Analyzing this intrusion is *A History of the Warfare of Science with Theology in Christendom* by Andrew Dickson White, a professor of history at Cornell University. In this troubling work, published in 1895, White recounts how the church (or dogmatic theology) battled against the fields of astronomy, geology, anthropology, chemistry, physics, and medicine as these disciplines were developing from embryonic beginnings into established disciplines. For example, theologians rejected the cosmological view that the earth is a sphere. Instead, they contended that the earth was flat like a pancake. In 1522, this flat-earth view was crushed by the return of a sea-faring expedition that had been led by Ferdinand Magellan, a Portuguese explorer, prior to his death in the Philippines. Setting sail from Europe in 1519, the expedition proved the sphericity of earth by circumnavigating it. Theologians were left with egg on their faces. The most famous battle between science and theology took place in the realm of astronomy. Theologians believed the sun revolved around the earth. But astronomers such as Galileo and Copernicus taught that the earth revolved around the sun. Roman Catholic and Protestant theologians denounced savagely this heliocentric theory. Martin Luther, arguing that Joshua commanded the sun and not the earth to stand still, referred to Copernicus as a fool. Today the heliocentric theory is universally accepted. Again, theologians were left with egg on their faces.

What is my point? The church has sashayed into areas—such as the physical sciences—where it has no expertise. In a similar way the church has seen fit to throw its weight around in the area of human sexuality. It has constructed what can be labeled a bourgeois sexual morality for church members. The term *bourgeois* is French and designates what sociologists refer to as the middle class (known collectively as the *bourgeoisie*). The term also refers to the typically conventional beliefs, attitudes, and practices of the middle class. Many Christians, particularly those living in the Deep South and in the small towns of America, are of the bourgeoisie. As members of the middle class they tend not to reason analytically. They believe but do not think. Instead, they let others do their thinking for them. They tend to swallow hook, line, and sinker what authoritative spokesmen for religion teach. Thus bourgeois Catholics reason: "The pope teaches that clerical celibacy is the will of God. Therefore clerical celibacy is the will of God. The matter is settled and no questions are to be asked." Or "The Catholic catechism teaches that masturbation is wrong. Therefore masturbation is wrong. The matter is settled and no questions are to be asked."

Whereas bourgeois Catholics listen to the pope and study the catechism, bourgeois Protestants worship before the altar of biblical fundamentalism. They view the Bible as a compilation of norms to direct human behavior. They believe that by consulting the Bible they can discover which sexual behaviors are right and which ones are wrong. But any person who pursues this rulebook approach encounters a problem. The Bible has no comprehensive systematic treatment of sexual matters. In fact, the Bible is a phantasmagoria—a runaway carousel—of sexual behaviors and norms.

- Abraham, the father of Jews and Arabs, allowed his wife—a woman named Sarah—to engage in hanky-panky with the pharaoh of Egypt (Gen 12).

- This same Sarah provided Abraham with a maid named Hagar so that he could impregnate her and thereby provide himself a male heir (Gen 16:1–5).

- Lot offered his daughters to the men of Sodom for them to rape (Gen 18 and 19).

- Tamar, posing as a harlot, seduced her father-in-law (Gen 38:12–26).

- David, Israel's greatest king, committed adultery with Bathsheba (2 Sam 11).

- Solomon, a Jewish monarch known for wisdom, had seven hundred wives plus a harem of three hundred mistresses (1 Kgs 11:3).

- Rahab, a harlot (Josh 2), was later viewed as a progenitrix of Jesus (Matt 1:5).

- Cult prostitutes plied their services inside Solomon's temple (2 Kgs 23:7).

- Jesus equated the libido with lust and asserted that any man who experiences sexual desire while looking at a woman thereby commits adultery with her in his heart (Matt 5:28). It was better to tear your eye out and throw it away than to allow this to happen (Matt 5:29)!

- Paul opined that it was a good thing for a man not to touch a woman (1 Cor 7:1).

- Yet the Song of Solomon in the Old Testament is a bucolic sex manual manifesting a preoccupation with female breasts (Song 1:13, 4:5, 7:3, 8:1, 8:8).

By now I, the person writing this book, have lived a long, long time. A lot of water has passed under the bridge. In my seventies, I have watched for decades the passing stream of life with all of its joys, expectations, frustrations, sorrows, and tragedies. While pondering this passing stream I have seen moral-religious beliefs collide with the slings and arrows of outrageous fortune: "It's easy," a parent may say, by way of example, "to be opposed to abortion until your fourteen-year-old daughter tells you she is pregnant." And while watching this passing stream I have met and talked with scores of middle-class church members who in their youth were socialized into the bourgeois sexual morality propagated by Roman Catholic and Protestant ethicists. Some middle-class church members have no trouble with this bourgeois sexual morality. But others—sincere and well-intentioned—are tormented by it. I have met teenagers tormented by their desire to masturbate. I have met middle-aged husbands tormented by the demands and boredom of lifelong monogamy. I have met widows tormented because they had an "affair" with a married man. They are steeped in sadness and guilt because—so they believe—they have committed adultery. The pages that follow have been written particularly for these tormented bourgeois Christians. I will be contending that they do not have to accept everything the church has taught about human sexuality. Some of the church's teachings in this area are wrong and have psychologically damaged people. Parenthetically, who granted to the church the right to regulate human sexuality? And parenthetically with regard to the Roman Catholic Church, does an unmarried and celibate clergy have anything to say about human sexuality that is worth listening to? Who knows? Maybe the Christian church has no more business attempting to regulate people's sex lives than attempting to regulate people's diet or sleeping habits.

In struggling for an enlightened approach to human sexuality, I suggest that we turn not to the catechisms or to biblical fundamentalism but to philosophy. And I suggest we heed that area of philosophy known as casuistry: the resolving of questions about conduct by pondering and appealing to ethical principles. I am aware that in some circles casuistry has fallen into disfavor. This is unfortunate for we are moral creatures. The late Ernst Troeltsch, a German philosopher-theologian, was right in contending that we are endowed with moral intuitions (not to be equated with religious intuitions). Thus, reasoning about moral questions is a part of being human. Reflective individual choice is an inescapable responsibility in moral living.

Furthermore, I suggest that we pay particular attention to a man named John Stuart Mill. I concede that in our time John Stuart Mill is not a household name. He was a kind, nineteenth-century English economist, philosopher, and social reformer. At one time a member of Parliament, he wrote extensively on economics and politics. In 1859, he published an influential political-philosophical work entitled *On Liberty*. In this treatise he was concerned with the roles government and society play in people's lives. To what extent, he asked, should people's actions be controlled by governmental authority and by the collective opinion of society? As far as their behavior is concerned, should people submit to the tyranny of the majority? In struggling with these questions Mill advanced what has come to be known as the harm principle: "The only purpose for which power can be rightfully exercised over any member of a civilized community, against his will, is *to prevent harm* to others."[1] In other words, the crucial question in determining the rightness or wrongness of conduct is: By his action is a person (or persons) harming someone else? According to Mill, "The only part of the conduct of anyone for which he is amenable to society is that which concerns others. In the part which merely concerns himself, his independence is, of right, absolute."[2]

Mill's harm principle, I wish to contend, can be modified and applied to sexual behavior. To wit: *The only circumstance under which society has a right to condemn and to prohibit a given sexual behavior is to prevent a person from doing harm to others.* I am not suggesting that this modified harm principle applies felicitously to sexual behavior that some people find aesthetically repulsive: for example, gay parades in New Orleans, or the viewing of lewd pornography, or the absorbing of visual sewage on Jerry Springer television programs, or the antics of a Cancun bacchanalia. This harm principle does, I believe, proscribe behaviors such as pedophilia, rape, sexual battery, and incest. Behaviors such as rape and incest do not provoke controversy as to their rightness or wrongness.

But some behaviors do provoke controversy. People have honest differences of opinion. I am thinking particularly of masturbation, homosexuality, fornication, adultery, and prostitution. In the discussion that follows I intend to apply the harm principle to these five areas. In making these applications I am not writing for the morally obtuse or the morally indifferent. Instead, I am writing for those who are morally sensitive and morally serious.

NOTES

1. John Stuart Mill, *On Liberty* (Indianapolis: Bobbs-Merrill Publishing, 1956), 13.

2. Ibid.

CHAPTER 3

Masturbation and the Harm Principle

Masturbation refers to a man or a woman stimulating his or her own sexual organs (penis, breasts, vagina, clitoris) in order to induce sexual pleasure—pleasure climaxing in orgasm. According to studies by behavioral researcher Alfred Kinsey and others, by age twenty more than 90 percent of men and more than 30 percent of women have masturbated. By age forty, more than 95 percent of men and more than 80 percent of women have masturbated at some time in their lives.[1] Thus masturbation—a taboo subject—is a practice most people engage in but nobody talks about.

Autoeroticism, self-pleasuring, and onanism are oblique, euphemistic terms for masturbation. These terms, however, are unknown to male adolescents. Instead, they use earthy expressions such as "jacking off" or "fucking my fist." This last expression focuses on the way a man masturbates. A man masturbates by wrapping his hand around his penis and then rhythmically rubbing his penis's shaft upward and downward until he experiences orgasm. The closer a man comes to climax the more swiftly he rubs his penis in an upward-downward motion. At the moment of orgasm his penis ejaculates semen.

A woman commonly masturbates by stimulating her clitoris with one finger or by inserting one or more fingers into her vagina. In the

1970s Shere Hite, a researcher of female sexuality, surveyed more than three thousand women concerning their sexual behavior. This survey, the results of which were published in book form under the title *The Hite Report*, involved asking women to complete questionnaires that included such inquiries as "Do you enjoy masturbating?" and "How do you masturbate?" The latter question received such answers as:

> I use my hands and my imagination, and have probably tried every imaginable position and motion—the basic stimulation remains the same. I use my finger to stimulate the clitoris, sometimes inserting another finger into my vagina at the same time. I touch only my genital area when I masturbate, because I am not stimulated by touching my body in general, as I am if my partner touches me all over.[2]

> I usually lie down, with my legs apart, maybe my knees up, I touch myself very gently, especially the inside of my thighs, then proceed to manipulate my clitoris directly with the middle finger of my right hand. I start slowly around my clitoris, and lubricate it with saliva or soap if necessary (soap if in a tub). I make my whole body "vibrate" by tensing my arm and moving it back and forth as fast as possible. I stop ever so often, especially if I'm near climax, so I can enjoy the period of arousal. My whole body moves rapidly upon reaching orgasm, and my pelvic area moves spasmodically up and down. Otherwise I lie quite still except for my hand moving. (24)

> When I masturbate, I begin by massaging the area of my clitoris with my whole hand. The massaging is usually soft to begin with, and it gets harder as I get more and more excited. I usually rub my fingertips back and forth over the sides of my clitoris because when I rub the tip of my clitoris the sensations are so strong that they are almost painful. I prefer that the rhythm of these movements be fairly constant, but I like to speed them up or slow them down as I desire. When I am having sex with a partner, I try to get him to duplicate these methods that I use when I masturbate. (29)

Thus masturbation, usually done in private (which explains why moralists refer to it as the "solitary vice"), is mankind's most prevalent sexual practice. It is more common than male-female (penile-vaginal) sexual intercourse. The reality is that every day around the world millions of boys, girls, men, and women masturbate.

This observation about the universality of masturbation is supported by the vast amount of anthropological and zoological research that was done in the later part of the nineteenth century and the early part of the twentieth. This research revealed, to quote from Thomas Laqueur's book entitled *Solitary Sex*, that not only was masturbation

> nearly universal among the young—this had long been feared and known—but that it was practiced by all people everywhere, under an enormous range of circumstances, and by just about every animal one cared to observe as well. Horses and Welsh ponies, bears and ferrets, dogs, cats, apes, skunks, and deer all did it. So did the Balinese, Egyptians, Hottentots, Indians, Tamils, Kaffirs, Basuto, Chinese, and Japanese, not to speak of students, male and female, in the best schools as well as the reformatories of Europe.[3]

Moreover, men of letters such as Jean-Jacques Rousseau, John Ruskin, Walt Whitman, and Andre Gide have seen fit to leave literary accounts of their masturbatory experiences. And A. W. Richard Sipe, a former Roman Catholic priest and the author of *Celibacy in Crisis*, contends that masturbation is the most common and frequently used sexual behavior of celibate priests. Sipe estimates that 80 percent of Catholic priests masturbate on occasion, some with regularity.[4]

Across the centuries, however, moralists have condemned masturbation, despite its universality. Disapproval is implied in the word itself. Etymologists believe "masturbation" is a combination of the Latin noun *manus*, which means "hand," and the Latin verb *stuprare*, which means "to defile." If this word derivation is correct, it follows that "masturbation" is a pejorative term meaning "defilement with the hand." Parenthetically, contemporary discussions about sexuality abound with pejorative expressions. Consider such terms as sodomy, lesbianism, and adultery. And contemporary sexuality discussions are replete with loaded expressions such as "having an affair" and "cheating on one's spouse."

In grappling with the rightness or wrongness of masturbation (also negatively referred to as self-abuse and self-pollution), some well-intentioned Christians, as I previously observed, appeal to the Bible. They view the Bible as a moral rulebook. But Christians of this rulebook persuasion are hard-pressed to find in the Bible a right-or-wrong rule about masturbation. Indeed, they are hard-pressed to find *any* explicit reference in the Bible to masturbation.

The biblical story about Onan (Gen 38:1–11) is cited time and again as an anti-masturbation episode. To make sense of this passage one must understand the Old Testament concept of levirate marriage. According to the Old Testament, if a husband died and left no son, the deceased husband's brother was expected to marry and impregnate his deceased brother's widow. By fathering an infant with his widowed sister-in-law and by giving the infant his brother's name, he would insure that his deceased brother's name would "not be blotted out of Israel." This man's responsibility to marry his brother's widow is spelled out in Deut 25:5–6 as follows: "When brothers reside together, and one of them dies and has no son, the wife of the deceased shall not be married outside the family to a stranger. Her husband's brother shall go in to her, taking her in marriage, and performing the duty of a husband's brother to her, and the firstborn whom she bears shall succeed to the name of the deceased brother, so that his name may not be blotted out of Israel."

When the Old Testament was translated from Hebrew into Latin, the Hebrew word *yaban* (the husband's brother) was rendered by the Latin *levir* (brother). Thus from the Latin word *levir* comes the term levirate marriage.

Returning to the Onan story: Gen 38:1–10 tells of a man named Judah who had two sons. One was named Er; the other was named Onan. Judah arranged a marriage between Er and a woman named Tamar. Er— at an early age—died childless. Thus Tamar was left a widow without a son to continue the name of her deceased husband. The law of levirate marriage mandated that Onan, Er's brother, marry Tamar. As just explained, by fathering a child who would be named Er, Onan would prohibit his brother's name from being "blotted out of Israel" (Deut 25:6). Judah therefore commanded Onan to take the wife of his deceased brother. Onan obeyed his father, but whenever he had sex with Tamar he allowed his semen to spill on the ground (Gen 38:9). Onan possibly did this so that some day he would inherit the wealth of an heirless, deceased brother. However, God punished Onan for spilling his ejaculation. What Onan "did was displeasing in the sight of the Lord, and he put him to death also" (Gen 38:10).

Moralists have condemned Onan's puzzling behavior as an act of masturbation. This interpretation has produced a synonym for masturbation: onanism. Yet the Genesis text does not state "Onan masturbated while having sex with Tamar." Instead, the text asserts that he allowed his semen to spill on the ground. This is an instance of *coitus interruptus* (literally: interrupted sexual intercourse), a Latin phrase referring to the intentional withdrawal of the penis from the vagina before orgasm. Its purpose is to prevent semen ejaculation into the vagina. Thus the Onan episode has nothing to do with masturbation. I repeat: Masturbation is not explicitly mentioned in the Bible. I emphasize this because Christian moralists have sought to condemn masturbation by appealing to "holy Scripture." And they have repeatedly viewed masturbation as an evil deed offensive to God. Consider, for example, the view of the thirteenth-century Dominican monk Thomas Aquinas, who authored a massive theological treatise entitled the *Summa Theologica*. In this work the Angelic Doctor, a title given to Aquinas, spelled out four types of lust that are particularly abhorrent because they are contrary to right reason and to nature. These four manifestations of abhorrent lust are: (1) bestiality (copulation with animals), (2) homosexuality, (3) deviation from the "natural manner of coitus" (evidently human copulation other than in the missionary position, that is, the man on top of the woman), and (4) masturbation.[5] In a similar vein the *New Catholic Encyclopedia* asserts: "It has been the constant and clear teaching of the Church from principles found in Holy Scripture that masturbation is a serious sin that will keep one from heaven. . . . The Church teaches that the sexual function is meant by God to serve primarily for the begetting of children. Therefore, any activation of it outside the proper state of marriage is seriously inordinate and sinful."[6] And the recently published Roman Catholic catechism declares: "Both the Magisterium of the Church, in the course of a constant tradition, and the moral sense of the faithful have been in no doubt and have firmly maintained that masturbation is an intrinsically and gravely disordered action."[7] Through ideological osmosis ("ideas have legs"), the Roman Catholic disapproval of masturbation has seeped into other branches of Christendom.

Parenthetically, Roman Catholic moralists have written more extensively about sexual topics (such as masturbation) than have Protestant moralists. Protestant moralists tend to avoid sexual issues. For example, the late Paul Ramsey of Princeton University wrote a book entitled *Basic Christian Ethics*, a classic in the realm of Christian morality. But alas! In Ramsey's book human sexuality is dealt with on two pages in a section entitled "The Restraint of Sin."[8]

Prior to the eighteenth century, masturbation was a harmless, marginal issue. Ancient doctors (such as Hippocrates and Galen) as well as medieval doctors either ignored masturbation or viewed it with indifference. References in literary works (diaries, theological treatises, sermons, essays) to the "solitary vice" are few and far between. When condemned by moralists it was on religious grounds. But the eighteenth century witnessed a dramatic—some would say a hysterical—change. Suddenly masturbation came to be viewed as an injurious, self-abusive practice that damaged both mind and body. The stimulus for this revised attitude toward masturbation was the publication in England (during the century's first quarter) of an eighty-eight-page document bearing the cumbersome title of *Onanism; or the Heinous Sin of Self Pollution, and all its Frightful Consequences, in both SEXES Considered, with Spiritual and Physical Advice to those who have already injured themselves by this abominable practice. And seasonable Admonition to the Youth of the Nation of both SEXES.* With the publication of this book the word onanism (at the time a neologism) was born. The identity of *Onanism*'s author is uncertain. Parenthetically, facsimile reproductions of this book are available through the Garland Publishing Company of New York. But a word to the wise: the text with its antique spelling is not easy to read. Today *Onanism* is viewed as a work of medical quackery. In the eighteenth century, however, it was taken seriously. Masturbation was presented in *Onanism* as a physical-medical problem: a heinous sin of self-pollution and an unnatural act by which people defile their bodies. In the reasoning about masturbation medicine replaced religion and morality. Ironically, this conception of masturbation as a destructive activity with terrible consequences is in sharp contrast to the frivolous attitude toward masturbation encountered in Jonathan Swift's *Gulliver's Travels*, a literary work also coming from the early part of the eighteenth century. In *Gulliver's Travels* masturbation is treated in a flippant manner. For example, in the first chapter the reader encounters such phrases as "My good Master Mr. *Bates*" followed by "my good master *Bates*."

According to eighteenth-century medical opinion, semen was associated with male virility. Males, it was believed, possessed limited amounts of semen. Thus masturbation was both unwise and dangerous because it robbed men of their physical powers. Consequently, sperm ejaculation depleted a male's energy reservoir; masturbators became lethargic.[9]

The eighteenth-century's anti-masturbation views passed undiminished into the nineteenth century. Sir James Paget, Queen Victoria's surgeon, viewed masturbation as "so nasty a practice; an uncleanness, a filthiness forbidden by God and despised by men."[10] Even cartoons were employed to convey anti-masturbation messages. Observe the appearance of the masturbator portrayed in a cartoon in Emery C. Abbey's *The Sexual System and Its Derangements*, a book published in 1875 in Buffalo, New York.

16-year-old masturbator, left;
21-year-old abstainer, right.

50-year-old masturbator, left;
70-year-old abstainer, right.

Possibly the most extensively read anti-masturbation book of the late nineteenth century was *What a Young Boy Ought to Know*.[11] This book, initially published in 1897, was written by Sylvanus Stall, a clergyman. The first several pages of Stall's book contain photographs of high-profile, dignified clergymen wearing high collars and sporting mutton-chop whiskers. One is a photograph of none other than Anthony Comstock, an anti-pornography zealot par excellence and the founder of the New York Society for the Suppression of Vice. Comstock is the person for whom the Comstock Act, passed in 1873, was named. This act, which made Comstock a special investigatory agent of the post office, made it a federal crime to send "obscene, lewd, or lascivious" publications through the mail. One by one these photographed divines commend Stall's book (thereby giving the book dignity and respectability, and deflecting any suspicion of erotic intent on the part of the author or publisher). *What a Young Boy Ought to Know*, rooted in the widely accepted medical beliefs of the time, purports to be a series of chats with a youngster named Harry. These excerpts reflect the view that masturbation has a debilitating effect on a person who engages in the "solitary vice." Indeed, so the Reverend Stall informs Harry, masturbation leads to all kinds of dire disasters.

> My Dear Friend Harry: No boy can toy with the exposed portions of his reproductive system without finally suffering very serious consequences. In the beginning it may seen to a boy a trifling matter, and yet from the very first his conscience will tell him that he is doing something that is very wrong. It is on this account that a boy who yields to such an evil temptation will seek a secluded, solitary place, and it is because of this fact that it is called the "solitary vice." Because the entire being of the one who indulges in this practice is debased and polluted by his own personal act it is also called "self-pollution." It is also called "Onanism," because for a similar offense, nearly four thousand years ago, God punished Onan with death (Genesis xxxviii, 3–10). This sin is also known by another name, and is called "masturbation," a word which is made from two Latin words which mean "To pollute by the hand." Each of these words tells something of the vile character of this sin.[12]

The Reverend Stall continues with warnings about death, idiocy, and becoming like Satan:

> In this as in other things, "To be forewarned is to be forearmed." Every young boy should be properly informed upon this subject, for even those who may be safely guarded from defilement of thought and life from outward influences are nevertheless exposed to those inward physical conditions which may produce local irritation and disease, and where such a diseased condition is ignorantly permitted to continue, masturbation soon becomes a fixed habit, and is likely to be practiced with such violence that idiocy, and even death, may, and often does come speedily. Nothing so much favors the continuance and spread of this awful vice as ignorance, and only by being early and purely taught on this important subject can the coming boys and men be saved from the awful consequences which are ruining morally, mentally, and physically thousands of boys every year.
>
> As I have already said, one of the first things which a boy does who undertakes to practice this vice is to seek solitude. From the very first his conscience disapproves, and so he cannot engage in the evil which he proposes to himself without violating his moral sense. Indeed, his moral nature is the first to suffer. This, my dear boy, is an important fact, and if you were ever to fall a victim to this vice, you would find that even with the first sense of guilt there would come a spirit of rebellion against God and against your parents. You would soon begin to call into question the wisdom and goodness of God. Your pleasure in good books, in religious instruction, in the Sunday-School, the Bible, the Church, and all holy things would rapidly diminish. You would soon find in your heart a rebellious feeling which would lead you to be disobedient, cross, irritable, and reproachful. You would begin to lose faith in all that is good, and as you persisted in your sin, you would grow less and less like Jesus and more and more like Satan. (99–101)

Harry is informed that masturbators become shy and pull their caps down so as to hide their eyes:

> My Dear Friend Harry: If I had time there are many things I would like to tell you concerning the way in which the effects of vice are manifested upon the moral nature and are seen in the lives of sinning boys and men; but I must hasten on, lest you weary.

After great changes have been effected in the boy's character, and the bright, frank, happy, and obedient boy has become the fretful, irritable, stolid, and reticent boy, and when he can no longer look people squarely and frankly in the face, but seeks to avoid meeting people, pulls his cap down so as to hide his eyes, and goes about with a shy and guilty bearing, then changes which are mental and physical may be confidently expected. (102–3)

Masturbators, Harry is informed, have poor digestion and flabby muscles.

While the nerves are thus being ruined, the mind is also suffering. The bright boy that stood at the head of the class is gradually losing his power to comprehend and retain his lessons. His memory fails him. His mind begins to lack grasp and grip. He cannot, as formerly, take hold and hold fast. Gradually he loses his place and drops back toward the foot of his class. He slowly but surely ceases to be positive and self-reliant. He no longer has his accustomed pleasure in the vigorous romp, the hearty laugh, and good fellowship which characterize a boy with a vigorous mind and a strong body.

While these moral and mental changes are taking place, the physical effects do not stop with the nerves. The health gradually declines. The eyes lose their luster. The skin becomes sallow. The muscles become flabby. There is an unnatural languor. Every little effort is followed by weariness. There is a great indifference to exertion. Work becomes distasteful and irksome. He complains of pain in the back; of headache and dizziness. The hands become cold and clammy. The digestion becomes poor, the appetite fitful. The heart palpitates. He sits in a stooping position, becomes hollow-chested, and the entire body, instead of enlarging into a strong, manly frame, becomes wasted, and many signs give promise of early decline and death.

These, my dear friend Harry, are some of the more prominent symptoms and effects of masturbation in boys and young men when the habit is frequently indulged, or after being continued for a period. (104–5)

Masturbation can lead to imbecility and insanity:

You will see, from what I have said, that this secret vice is attended with most serious consequences. But I have not yet told you the worst. If persisted in, masturbation will not only undermine, but completely overthrow the health. If the body is naturally strong, the mind may give way first, and in extreme cases imbecility and insanity may, and often do come as the inevitable result. (106)

Worst of all, masturbator's children suffer:

> But the consequences which result from masturbation do not stop with the boy who practices it, nor with his parents, brothers and sisters, friends and relatives, but where such a boy lives to become a man, if he marries, and should become a father, his children after him must suffer to some measurable degree the results of his sin. If his life has disqualified him for thrift, and his children on this account are born in poverty this would be one of the results which they would suffer. But if his physical powers have been impaired by vice, or any other cause, he cannot transmit perfect or as good physical, mental, and moral powers to his children as he otherwise might. For neither physically nor financially can a man transmit or give to his children that which he does not himself possess. As in grain so in human life, if the quality of the grain which is sown in the field is poor, the grain that grows from it will be inferior. When a boy injures his reproductive powers, so that when a man his sexual secretion shall be of an inferior quality, his offspring will show it in their physical, mental, and moral natures. (112–13)

To partially recapitulate: According to the Reverend Sylvanus Stall (who personifies accepted beliefs about the "solitary vice" held in the eighteenth, nineteenth, and early twentieth centuries), masturbation leads to imbecility, insanity, and death. It causes eyes to lose their luster, skin to become sallow, and muscles to become flabby. Masturbation produces headaches, poor digestive systems, and hollow chests. A masturbator is fretful, irritable, and cannot look people squarely in the face (which explains why he pulls his cap down over his eyes). He questions the wisdom and goodness of God, loses pleasure in holy things, and fathers children who are mentally and physically inferior. In view of such consequences, no wonder masturbation was condemned in previous centuries! I have deliberately quoted Sylvanus Stall extensively because these quotations capture vividly the attitude toward masturbation that existed in this country and Europe until recently. Indeed, in my own youth I was told that masturbation caused a person to go crazy. Since bourgeois sexual morality condemns masturbation, homosexuality, fornication, and adultery (these last three topics I will deal with momentarily), the end result is that sexual expression or pleasure is denied to all but the married.

But fields such as medicine and psychology move on to new views and revised positions. Beliefs once accepted as true are subsequently abandoned, as is the case of the Victorian view of masturbation. Today's rejection of the Reverend Stall's hysteria against the "solitary vice" is evident in the following observation by Benjamin J. Sadock, a physician with the New York University School of Medicine: "No scientific evidence supports the idea that masturbation causes physical or mental disease of any kind."[13] And as Richard Sipe has observed in his book *Celibacy in Crisis*,

> Quite simply, under ordinary circumstances, masturbation can be a natural, healthy, unselfish act, expected at any stage of life as a part of the process of growth, self-definition, and normal sexual function. . . . The claims that masturbation can be virtuous may seem revolutionary at first blush, but only the unreflective or inexperienced clinician or moralist can hold that it is intrinsically evil and inherently unhealthy.[14]

If this be true, then obviously the time has come for masturbation to be rescued from the pages of church catechisms and from the hands of divines like the late Sylvanus Stall. A first step in this rescuing effort is to realize there is nothing wrong or sinful about the masturbatory act. To masturbate is as innocent and non-sinful as playing hopscotch or eating a bacon-and-tomato sandwich. At the same time, a change in terminology is sorely needed. A total discontinuance of the term *masturbation* (pollution with the hand) would be fortunate. Sex therapists have suggested substitute terms such as self-pleasuring and self-gratification. But terminology changes slowly. For the foreseeable future we are stuck with masturbation, a derogatory word.

Instead of being corrupting or polluting, self-gratification is biologically normal, wholesome, and healthy. It is the means by which both sexes discover and explore their sexuality. Through masturbation boys and girls discover an insight moralists and theologians ignore, namely, *sex feels good*. Sex is pleasurable. The female clitoris is evidence of sexual pleasure in that it has no other function than to evoke pleasurable sensations. The word *clitoris* comes from the Greek word for key. Hence the clitoris is for women the key that opens them up to sexual pleasure. The blissful sensation of orgasm (which masturbation makes possible) was designed and brought into being by God. Orgasm, theologians and moralists forget, is God's idea. Not Satan's.

I want us now to apply the harm principle—the only circumstance under which society has a right to condemn and to prohibit a given sexual behavior is to prevent a person from doing harm to others)—to masturbation. Imagine a teenage boy masturbating in his bedroom at night.[15] Or visualize a middle-aged divorcee or widow masturbating before she goes to sleep. Or a sixty-year-old widower doing the same thing. *What harm have they done to others? What harm have they done to themselves?* I can think of none. Society's pathologizing and condemnation of masturbation is as irrational as it is unjustified. Rarely do people who condemn masturbation have their feet held to the fire by being asked: *Why* is masturbation immoral? When they try to answer this query objectively, they encounter what I am labeling the disapproval dilemma. They can't come up with a convincing answer to the *why* question: *Why* is masturbation wrong? To construct an airtight, unanswerable reason for the wrongness of masturbation is impossible.

In a utopian world, self-pleasuring would be viewed as an innocent act. But we do not live in that kind of world. Instead, we live in a world in which people revel in being judgmental and condemnatory. I predict (with regret) that centuries from now the church and moralists will still be condemning self-pleasuring. Consequently, the challenge each person faces today is the challenge of becoming morally autonomous while transcending the condemnatory society within which he or she lives: "As far as moral decisions are concerned, I'm going to paddle my own boat. I'm not going to allow others to decide for me what is right and what is wrong. I'll make those decisions myself." Obviously, to adopt this stance requires both moral courage and a sense of independence. I contend that a person possessing both characteristics can (without shame) rejoice in self-pleasuring, viewing masturbation as a human blessing, a gift from God, and a means for exploring and satisfying human sexuality.

NOTES

1. This quotation is from an article entitled "Masturbation" on pp. 482–83 in volume 18 of *Encyclopedia Americana* (Danbury: Scholastic Library Publishing, Inc., 2004). The article is by Benjamin J. Sadock, M.D., of the New York University of Medicine.

2. Shere Hite, *The Hite Report* (New York: Macmillan Publishing Company, 1976), 21.

3. Thomas Laqueur, *Solitary Sex* (New York: Zone Books, 2003), 66.

4. A. W. Richard Sipe, *Celibacy in Crisis* (New York: Brunner-Routledge, 2003), 57.

5. *Summa Theologica*, II-II, cliv. 11. These four vices are discussed in Derrick Sherwin Bailey, *Sexual Relations in Christian Thought* (New York: Harper & Brothers, 1959), 160–61. They are also discussed in Paul Abramson and Steven Pinkerton, *With Pleasure* (Oxford: Oxford University Press, 2002), 21.

6. J. J. Farraher, "Masturbation," *New Catholic Encyclopedia* (New York: McGraw-Hill Book Company, 1967), 9:438.

7. *Catechism of the Catholic Church* (Liguori, Mo.: Liguori Publications, 1994), 564, paragraph 2351.

8. Paul Ramsey, *Basic Christian Ethics* (New York: Charles Scribner's Sons, 1950), 328–29.

9. Two later reformers who opposed masturbation for health reasons were Sylvester Graham, the inventor of graham crackers, and John Kellogg of cornflakes fame. These men recommended cold baths, fresh air, exercise, Bible reading, and bland food (particularly corn flakes and graham crackers) as masturbation deterrents. Such quaint techniques to quell masturbatory desires can be referred to as "corn-flakes therapy." John Kellogg had an older brother named J. H. Kellogg who was a medical doctor. This older brother published a book entitled *Plain Facts for Old and Young* (Burlington, VT: Segner and Condit, 1881). In this book on pages 428 and 429, Dr. Kellogg condemned self-pollution (masturbation) with the following words: "The sin of self-pollution is one of the vilest, the basest, and the most degrading that a human being can

commit. It is worse than beastly. Those who commit it place themselves far below the meanest brute that breathes. The most loathsome reptile, rolling in the slush and slime of its stagnant pool, would not demean itself thus. A boy who is thus guilty [of self-pollution] ought to be ashamed to look into the eyes of an honest dog."

10. Thomas W. Laqueur, *Solitary Sex* (New York: Zone Books, 2003), 17.

11. Incidentally, the book's title is not *What a Young Boy and Girl Ought to Know*. Rather, the title refers to a "young boy." Nineteenth-century moralists were primarily concerned with male masturbation. Evidently, they did not know about dildoes and the possibility of female masturbation. Across the centuries women's sexual life and behavior has remained vague or unknown to most male writers on sexual ethics.

12. Sylvanus Stall, *What a Young Boy Ought to Know* (Philadelphia: The Vir Publishing Company, 1897), 97–98.

13. Sadock, "Masturbation," *Encyclopedia Americana*, 18:482.

14. Sipe, *Celibacy in Crisis*, 66, 72.

15. This act—for aesthetic reasons—should be done in private. I do not recommend imitating Diogenes the Cynic who, as recounted by Diogenes Laertius in his *Lives of the Eminent Philosophers*, masturbated in broad daylight in the Athenian agora (market place). Nor do I recommend imitating Pee-Wee Herman, who got into trouble in 1991 for masturbating in a movie theater.

CHAPTER 4

Homosexuality and the Harm Principle

Word Definitions and the Sodom Story

I propose that we begin this discussion by defining two terms: homosexuality and lesbianism. The former term, so common in our day, is a Johnny-come-lately, being less than a century and a half old. German psychiatrists of the nineteenth century coined the term *homosexualität*, which came into English as homosexuality. The prefix *homo* is derived from the Greek *homos* and means "the same." Thus "homosexuality" means "same sexuality" and designates the tendency to be attracted to members of one's own sex. Both males and females can be homosexuals. Some people erroneously think the term "homosexual" applies only to males. They reason as they do because they mistakenly think that the prefix *homo* is Latin (man) rather than Greek (*homos*, meaning "the same"). In colloquial speech a male homosexual is degradingly referred to as a homo, a gay, a queer, a fruit, a fag, and a pervert. More euphemistically, male homosexuals are sometimes called deviants and inverts.

Female homosexuals are known as lesbians. The etymology of this term is not obvious. It is derived from the name of an island: Lesbos.

With a population today of slightly more than one hundred thousand, Lesbos—located off the coast of Turkey—has the largest population of the Greek islands in the Aegean Sea. Occupied by the Greeks around 1050 B.C.E., Lesbos was the locale of a culture that excelled in lyric poetry, that is, poetry sung while accompanied by a lyre, a stringed musical instrument. One of these lyric poetesses was named Sappho. Although married and the mother of a daughter, Sappho—so her contemporaries reported—had a passionate friendship for and attraction toward young girls. This friendship led to her being identified as homosexual. From the name of the island on which Sappho lived has been coined the term *lesbianism*: a noun designating female homosexuality, that is, the sexual attraction of females to other females. Thus T. G. Johnson could write a brief monograph entitled *Sappho the Lesbian*.[1] In colloquial speech a female homosexual is degradingly referred to by such terms as dike or nancy.

Some of the world's most creative people, it must be acknowledged, have been homosexual. Part I of this book made reference to Socrates, the Athenian maverick who is one of the great personalities of Western philosophy. Socrates, although married, was also homosexual.

So was Michelangelo (1475–1564), the Italian sculptor and painter who embodied the highest artistic skills of the Renaissance. Like Socrates, Michelangelo was a maverick. Black-bearded and broken-nosed as a result of a student brawl, he was an eccentric bachelor with an explosive temper who usually wore workmen's clothes and lived simply. To this day people marvel at his *Pietá*, a marble statue portraying the dead Christ in the lap of the mourning Virgin Mary. And tourists from around the world visit Rome to view Michelangelo's painting *The Creation of Adam* on the ceiling of the Sistine Chapel and to view his artwork in the interior of the dome of St. Peter's Basilica.

Or consider Alan Turing, an Englishman who earned a Ph.D. in logic from Princeton University. As a young man Turing worked for the British Code and Cipher School at Bletchley during World War II, helping to decipher the German war code—a decipherment that was a major contribution to the defeat of Germany during the war. Turing was one of the founders of computer science (constructing a proto-computer known as ACE—Automatic Computing Engine) and wrote extensively on artificial intelligence. He was also a homosexual.

So was Oscar Wilde, the poet and dramatist. So was Ludwig Wittgenstein, the father of an influential philosophical movement known as logical positivism. So was Leonard Bernstein, the composer-conductor. So was Ludwig II of Bavaria, who built the fairy-tale castle of Neuschwanstein.

The names of creative homosexuals—persons of genius—could go on and on. Yet many have suffered savagely because of their sexual identity. For example, Alan Turing was convicted of engaging in homosexual acts and committed suicide while in his early forties as a result. Time and again homosexuals have been blasted. This condemnation broaches the question: Why? Why have societies been so condemning of homosexuality?

Societies that condemn homosexuality tend to be those influenced (at least in the past) by the Christian religion. It is easy to understand why the Christian religion has a condemning attitude toward homosexuality. Christians reason as follows: "The Bible is for us what the Koran is to Muslims: an inspired, foundational document. On more than one occasion the Bible affirms that homosexuality is wrong. Therefore, we have no choice but to condemn homosexuality because it is condemned in the Bible." Appealing to casuistry, I shall later question this line of reasoning. For the moment, however, I wish simply to acknowledge that the Bible *does* condemn homosexuality. This condemnatory stance goes all the way back to the Torah (the first five books of the Old Testament, which are sometimes referred to as the Law of Moses). Leviticus 18:22 asserts: "You shall not lie with a male as with a woman; it is an abomination." Similarly, Lev 20:13 declares: "If a man lies with a male as with a woman, both of them have committed an abomination; they shall be put to death; their blood is upon them." Those are strong words—homosexuals should be executed.

Across the centuries, however, the *locus classicus* (the classic place) to argue for divine condemnation of homosexuality is the Sodom episode

61

related in the book of Genesis. This Sodom story has contributed to our language the term sodomy, a synonym for homosexuality, and the term sodomite, a synonym for a homosexual. I shall now quote this episode in full because of the influential role it has played in reasoning about sexual morality. The text reads as follows:

> The two angels came to Sodom in the evening, and Lot was sitting in the gateway of Sodom. When Lot saw them, he rose to meet them, and bowed down with his face to the ground. He said, "Please, my lords, turn aside to your servant's house and spend the night, and wash your feet; then you can rise early and go on your way." They said, "No; we will spend the night in the square." But he urged them strongly; so they turned aside to him and entered his house; and he made them a feast, and baked unleavened bread, and they ate. But before they lay down, the men of the city, the men of Sodom, both young and old, all the people to the last man, surrounded the house; and they called to Lot, "Where are the men who came to you tonight? Bring them out to us, so that we may know them." Lot went out of the door to the men, shut the door after him, and said, "I beg you, my brothers, do not act so wickedly. Look, I have two daughters who have not known a man; let me bring them out to you, and do to them as you please; only do nothing to these men, for they have come under the shelter of my roof." But they replied, "Stand back!" And they said, "This fellow came here as an alien, and he would play the judge! Now we will deal worse with you than with them." Then they pressed hard against the man Lot, and came near the door to break it down. But the men inside reached out their hands and brought Lot into the house with them, and shut the door. And they struck with blindness the men who were at the door of the house, both small and great, so that they were unable to find the door. (Gen 19:1–11)

The story obviously draws upon Jewish folklore; its plot is easy to grasp. Lot, Abraham's nephew, settled in the city of Sodom. Two angels visited the city. Arriving in the evening, they were met at the city's gate by Lot. He urged them to accept the hospitality of his house. Before Lot and the angels retired for the night, the house was besieged by Sodomite citizens who demanded that the visitors be brought out to them in order that they might "know" them. Lot tried to dissuade the men by offering them his daughters. "Do to them as you please." The mob was thwarted in the end by the angels, who smote the mob with blindness. The next morning the angels led Lot and his family out of Sodom, and then God destroyed it with fire and brimstone rained down from heaven.

A consistent interpretive tradition—going back for at least two thousand years—contends that this unsavory episode concerns homosexuality. The Sodomite mob wanted to "know" the two visitors. The Hebrew verb "know" can refer to sexual intercourse and is so used in the Old Testament (Gen 4:1, 17, 25; 19:8; 24:16; 38:26; Jud 11:39; 19:25; 1 Sam 1:19; 1 Kgs 1:4). Thus—so traditional interpretation contends—the Sodomites wanted to have homosexual liaisons with Lot's visitors, whereupon Lot made the curious counterproposal of offering to allow the Sodomites to have heterosexual liaisons with his daughters.

Possibly the earliest interpreter to expressly accuse the Sodomites of homosexuality was Philo, a Jew who lived in Alexandria in Egypt and was a contemporary of Jesus and Saint Paul. Philo, familiar with Greek culture, was a voluminous author. Ten volumes are required in the Loeb Classical Library to duplicate and to translate his writings, which include a treatise entitled *On Abraham*. In this treatise Philo accuses the Sodomites of homosexual behavior:

> The land of the Sodomites, a part of the land of Canaan afterwards called Palestinian Syria, was brimful of innumerable iniquities, particularly such as arise from gluttony and lewdness, and multiplied and enlarged every other possible pleasure with so formidable a menace that it had at last been condemned by the Judge of All. The inhabitants owed this extreme licence to the never-failing lavishness of their sources of wealth, for, deep-soiled and well-watered as it was, the land had every year a prolific harvest of all manner of fruits, and the chief beginning of evils, as one has aptly said, is goods in excess. Incapable of bearing such satiety, plunging like cattle, they threw off from their necks the law of nature and applied themselves to deep drinking of strong liquor and dainty feeding and forbidden forms of intercourse. Not only in their mad lust for women did they violate the marriages of their neighbours, but also men mounted males without respect for the sex nature which

the active partner shares with the passive; and so when they tried to beget children they were discovered to be incapable of any but a sterile seed. Yet the discovery availed them not, so much stronger was the force of the lust which mastered them. Then, as little by little they accustomed those who were by nature men to submit to play the part of women, they saddled them with the formidable curse of a female disease. For not only did they emasculate their bodies by luxury and voluptuousness but they worked a further degeneration in their souls and, as far as in them lay, were corrupting the whole of mankind.[2]

Take notice of Philo's assertions: the Sodomites applied themselves to "forbidden forms of intercourse"; "men mounted males"; "little by little they [the Sodomites] accustomed those who were by nature men to submit to play the part of women." Consequently, Sodomites were guilty of "corrupting the whole of mankind."

Josephus, a Jewish historian of the first century who was also a voluminous writer, held a view of the Sodomites that is identical to Philo's. In Josephus's massive historical work *Antiquities of the Jews* he made this assertion about the angels who visited Lot: "Now when the Sodomites saw the young angels to be of beautiful countenances, and this to an extraordinary degree . . . they resolved themselves to enjoy those beautiful boys by force and violence" (I.xi.3).[3]

That Sodom's sin was sexual in nature is expressed in Jude, the next-to-last book in the New Testament. Verse seven in Jude declares that Sodom and Gomorrah "indulged in sexual immorality and pursued unnatural lust."

The church fathers (such as Clement of Alexandria, John Chrysostom, and Augustine of Hippo) held a view similar to that of Philo, Josephus, and Jude. Thus in his *City of God* Augustine opined: "After this promise, when Lot had escaped from Sodom, there came down from heaven a torrent of fire, and the whole region of that ungodly city was turned to ashes. For it was a place where sexual intercourse between males had become so commonplace that it received the licence usually extended by the law to other practices."[4]

The conclusion is obvious: early Judaic-Christian thinkers believed the Sodomites (whom they viewed as moral monsters) were annihilated because of their homosexual practices. Therefore, these thinkers denounced homosexuality on the basis of their understanding of the Sodom episode found in the Old Testament. But homosexuality is denounced also in the New Testament. Consider these New Testament quotations:

> Therefore God gave them up in the lusts of their hearts to impurity, to the degrading of their bodies among themselves. . . . Their women exchanged natural intercourse for unnatural, and in the same way also the men, giving up natural intercourse with women, were consumed with passion for one another. Men committed shameless acts with men and received in their own persons the due penalty for their error. (Rom 1:24–27)
>
> Do you not know that wrongdoers will not inherit the kingdom of God? Do not be deceived! Fornicators, idolaters, adulterers, male prostitutes, sodomites, thieves, the greedy, drunkards, revilers, robbers—none of these will inherit the kingdom of God. (1 Cor 6:9–10)
>
> Now we know that the law is good, if one uses it legitimately. This means understanding that the law is laid down not for the innocent but for the lawless and disobedient, for the godless and sinful, for the unholy and profane, for those who kill their fathers or mothers, for murderers, fornicators, sodomites, slave traders, liars, perjurers, and whatever else is contrary to the sound teaching. (1 Tim 1:8–10)

In these verses homosexuals are categorized with such villains as thieves, murderers, and slave traders. This biblical condemnation of homosexuality has—through ideological seepage—influenced secular law. By this I mean that political entities such as national and state governments have passed laws that reflect the Bible's antagonism toward homosexuality.

For example, one of the earliest accounts of English law is found in a document known as the *Fleta*. It is the first known legal writing in England to mention sodomy. Legal historians conjecture that this treatise comes from the later part of the thirteenth century (during the reign of Edward I). The *Fleta* proscribes that homosexuals are to be buried alive: "Those who have dealings with Jews or Jewesses, those who commit bestiality, and sodomists, are to be buried alive, after legal proof that they were taken in the act, and public conviction" (I.xxxvii.3).[5]

Another codification of English law was issued shortly after the *Fleta* and is called the *Britton*. In this codification the penalty for sodomy is spelled out as follows: "Let enquiry also be made of those who feloniously in time of peace have burnt others' corn or houses, and those who are attainted thereof shall be burnt. . . . The same sentence shall be passed upon sorcerers, sorceresses, renegades, sodomists, and heretics publicly convicted" (I.10).[6]

Alas for homosexuals: They are either to be buried or burned alive! It goes without saying that later English laws attenuated these draconian penalties. A prison term eventually became a common punishment for sodomy. Consider the prison term inflicted on Oscar Wilde, mentioned earlier as a homosexual. A graduate of Oxford, Wilde moved as a young man in his twenties to London, where his output of literary criticism, poetry, drama, and fiction was phenomenal. He was noted for his witticisms: "I can resist anything except temptation." To this day Wilde is revered in literary circles for his novel *The Picture of Dorian Gray*, a moral fable, and for plays such as *Lady Windermere's Fan* and *The Importance of Being Earnest*. In 1895, at the peak of his career as a dramatist, he had three plays running simultaneously in London. But in that same year he was accused of having a homosexual relationship with Lord Alfred Douglas, a young aristocrat. His accuser was Alfred Douglas's father. Wilde foolishly decided to sue for libel. In the ensuing trial Wilde was convicted of homosexuality and was sentenced to two years in prison at hard labor. On his release from prison Wilde was a broken man. He fled to France, where he lived the life of a bankrupt alcoholic. He died (of meningoencephalitis) in Paris in 1900 at the age of forty-six.

I am belaboring the insight that English common law adopted contemporary church doctrine. Sodomy became both a religious sin and a civil crime. This correlation of English law and biblical morality is evident in the observation of Sir William Blackstone, an eighteenth-century English jurist, that homosexuality is a "crime against nature," which "the voice of nature and of reason, and the express law of God, determine to be capital. Of which we have a signal instance, long before the Jewish dispensation, by the destruction of two cities by fire from heaven: so that this is a universal, not merely a provincial precept."[7] This just-quoted reference to Sodom and Gomorrah is found in Blackstone's monumental *Commentaries on the Laws of England*. In this Blackstone statement the laws of England and the "express law of God" or biblical morality (Sodom's destruction because of homosexuality) are blended together.

Likewise, the original thirteen American colonies had anti-sodomy laws. In this regard they walked in England's footsteps. In colonial law codes sodomy was referred to as an "unnatural sin" and an "offence against God."[8] All the states had anti-sodomy laws by 1960. Today many states have repealed them, with Illinois being the first to do so in 1961. However, approximately thirteen states still have anti-sodomy laws on the books. And so the city of Sodom, described in Genesis as one of the wicked cities of the Plain, continues to cast a shadow over American jurisprudence.[9]

Homosexuality: A Puzzle

Homosexuality is both a medical and a psychological puzzle. No one fully understands it. Researchers have sought to answer relevant questions, but answers have been hard to come by.

Consider the sensible question: What percentage of humankind is gay or lesbian? One would think this would be an easy question to answer. But researchers encounter obstacles when they seek to answer this question. Not surprisingly, some homosexuals, aware of the prejudice existing against gays and lesbians, hesitate or refuse to identify themselves as such. They would never participate in a survey seeking to determine the prevalence of homosexuality. In addition, the cultural context within which people live can influence the percentage who are homosexual. Homosexuality tends to increase among groups that do not have access to members of the opposite sex—groups such as prison inmates, soldiers, and the clergy of churches that require celibacy. Therefore, the best researchers can do is approximate. As Francis Mark

Mondimore has observed, "Assertations are frequently made about the proportion of people who are homosexual to a significant degree—for example, in the United States, 10 percent of men and 5 percent of women. In reality, such figures are rough estimates." Obtaining precise figures on how many people are homosexual is difficult to obtain because of the high degree of prejudice which exists against homosexuals. Understandably, many homosexuals do not reveal to others their sexual orientation. Dr. Mondimore further observed that studies suggest that the rate of homosexuality among women is about half the rate found among men.[10]

And then there is the vexing question: Why are some people homosexual? What is the etiology (the cause) of homosexuality? For decades this question has stirred debate. Is homosexuality a product of nature (biology) or is it a product of nurture (environment)? Are some people genetically programmed (wired) to be homosexuals? Or contrariwise, does society condition (encourage or teach) some people to be gay or lesbian? Or do some people deliberately choose to be homosexual?

Evidence can be cited to support all of these viewpoints. Consider, for example, the Sambia, a warrior society that inhabits the southeastern highlands of Papua New Guinea. Gilbert Herdt, an anthropologist, spent several years during the 1970s studying the Sambia, who are believed to be descendants of Asian people who traveled by boat thousands of years ago to colonize the islands of the South Pacific Ocean. Herdt observed that Papuan people (to whom he gave the name of Sambia, a pseudonym) practiced institutionalized homosexuality. Among the Sambia men semen was thought of as a masculine essence without which a boy would remain passive or listless. In other words, Sambia men believed that semen is the source of male masculinity and strength: "The more semen you have the more masculine you are." Yet young boys—prior to puberty—are incapable of semen ejaculation. To masculinize them requires some method of infusing them with semen. How can this absence-of-semen problem be solved? The Sambia "solve" this problem by encouraging pre-pubertal boys to perform fellatio (oral intercourse) on older boys. The younger boys swallow the older boys' ejaculated semen and by so doing infuse themselves with masculine energy derived from the ingested semen. All Sambia boys pass through a period of homosexual behavior as a necessary step on the road to manhood. Among the Sambia this homosexual period is transitory. On becoming adults Sambia men marry and become fathers.[11] However, "The Sambia are not unique in practicing ritualized homosexuality; additional examples can be found in Melanesia, Africa, and South America."[12] Athenian vase paintings and Platonic dialogues (such as the *Symposium*) that have come down to us from ancient Greece suggest that homosexuality was accepted and widely practiced among the Greeks. These just-cited instances support the theory that homosexuality is culturally determined.

Yet another body of evidence suggests that homosexuality is biologically based. This theory contends that some people are wired to be gays and lesbians. This theory also contends that homosexuality is as "natural" as heterosexuality. The physical or biological evidence for this viewpoint is beyond the scope of this book and is far beyond my professional expertise. Indeed, discussions of hormones, testosterone, and brain features such as the hypothalamus and pituitary gland are fiendishly difficult (or impossible) for lay persons to understand. Be that as it may, neuroscientists have probed into the biological underpinnings of homosexuality. Some neuroscientists contend that physiological differences exist between homosexual persons and heterosexual persons. Any reader of this book wishing to pursue further evidence of the biological basis for homosexuality would do well to read *A Natural History of Homosexuality* by Francis Mark Mondimore, a practicing psychiatrist and a member of the clinical faculty of the University of North Carolina at Chapel Hill. In his book Mondimore discusses, for example, Simon LeVay's 1991 study comparing the size of hypothalamic nuclei in homosexual men and in heterosexual men. LeVay discovered that this nucleus was smaller in gay men than in non-gay men. "This was the first structural brain difference between homosexual and heterosexual men ever described."[13] The occurrence of homosexuality among siblings also suggests that homosexuality is genetic in origin.

While writing this book I interviewed gays and lesbians, several of whom told me that during their adolescent years they gradually became aware—as one of them expressed it "that something wasn't right." They observed that other adolescents their age were sexually attracted to members of the opposite sex—boys to girls and girls to boys. But they were not. They were attracted to members of their own sex. This attraction was not welcomed. As one gay expressed it, "Being attracted to members of my own sex was for me a source of shame and guilt. I did everything within my power to deny and to suppress this attraction." In interviews I discovered that homosexuals raised within conservative-fundamentalist churches experienced excruciating feelings of sinfulness and self-hate as they awakened to their sexual identity. The psychological torment experienced by these adolescents has been captured by E. M. Forster in his novel *Maurice*. This novel, which lay unpublished for almost sixty years, has two main characters, both of whom are homosexuals. One is named Maurice; the other is named Clive. The men take opposite paths in dealing with their homosexuality. Maurice lives openly as a homosexual. Clive marries and attempts to suppress his homosexual inclinations. Forster writes as follows about the young Clive confronting his homoerotic impulse and thereby concluding his soul was damned.

> Clive had suffered little from bewilderment as a boy. His sincere mind, with its keen sense of right and wrong, had brought him the belief that he was damned instead. Deeply religious, with a living desire to reach God and to please Him, he found himself crossed at an early age by this other desire, obviously from Sodom. . . . He had in him the impulse that destroyed the City of the Plain. It should not ever become carnal, but why had he out of all Christians been punished with it?
>
> At first he thought God must be trying him, and if he did not blaspheme would recompense him like Job. He therefore bowed his head, fasted, and kept away from anyone whom he found himself inclined to like. His sixteenth year was ceaseless torture. He told no one, and finally broke down and had to be removed from school. During the convalescence he found himself falling in love with a cousin who walked by his bath chair, a young married man. It was hopeless, he was damned.[14]

I find myself sympathetic to Clive and I regret his conclusion that he was damned because he was a Sodomite, having a desire from Sodom, the destroyed City of the Plain. And I find myself sympathetic to the theory that many gays (like Clive) and lesbians have homoerotic impulses that are genetically imposed upon them. In other words, their homosexual identity is not a matter of personal choice. They did not wake up one day and glibly say, "I choose to be homosexual." Nor do I believe heterosexuals awake one morning and declare, "I choose to be heterosexual." To the contrary, their sexual orientation is inborn. Indeed, I have never met a heterosexual who could tell me *when, where, and under what circumstances he or she deliberately chose his or her sexual orientation.* To do that would be like expecting a heterosexual to relate when, where, and under what circumstances he or she chose his or her eye color or body height.

Some moralists, however, contend that homosexuals deliberately choose to be gay or lesbian. This view of homosexuality as a *chosen* (rather than a genetically imposed) lifestyle ignores a *why* question: In light of the heavy calumny, ridicule, and criticism heaped upon homosexuals, *why* would any person deliberately choose to be gay or lesbian? Across the years, homosexuals have been flagellated; they have had both physical and emotional pain inflicted upon them. Nazi Germany held them in contempt and sent them to death camps. At Sachsenhausen, Buchenwald, and other Nazi concentration camps, homosexuals were required to wear pink triangles to distinguish them from Jews (who wore yellow stars) and political prisoners (who wore red triangles). Nazi surgeons tried to rehabilitate homosexuals by castrating them.

In addition, the Roman Catholic Church in its current catechism asserts about homosexual acts:

> Basing itself on Sacred Scripture, which presents homosexual acts as acts of grave depravity, tradition has always declared that "homosexual acts are intrinsically disordered." They are contrary to natural law. They close the sexual act to the gift of life. They do not proceed from a genuine affective and sexual complementarity. Under no circumstances can they be approved.[15]

71

As though condemnation by the church was not enough, homosexuality has had stones thrown at it by the field of psychiatry. As previously observed, psychiatrists in Germany coined the term homosexuality. They viewed it as a mental illness. That homosexuality was caused by a dysfunctional relationship with one's parents was a theory frequently advanced. It was not until 1974 that the American Psychiatric Association removed homosexuality from the list of illnesses in its official *Diagnostic and Statistical Manual*.

And then there is Jerry Falwell, who opined that gays and lesbians were partly responsible for the destruction of New York's World Trade Center. On Pat Robertson's *700 Club* show the Reverend Falwell said about the tragedy: "I really believe that the pagans, and the abortionists, and the gays and the lesbians who are actively trying to make that an alternative lifestyle, the ACLU, People for the American Way—all of them who have tried to secularize America—I point the finger in their face and say, 'You helped this happen.'"[16]

And so homosexuals catch it from all sides. Returning to the issue of whether or not gays and lesbians choose to be homosexual, moralists in the Falwell tradition could reason as follows: "For the sake of argument, we will concede momentarily that homosexuals do not choose their orientation, but nonetheless we contend that they could choose not to capitulate to their inherited sexual orientation." In other words, such moralists might say, "If you are a homosexual, don't behave like one. Be chaste." This is the behavior recommended by the Roman Catholic Church. I quote again from its current catechism: "Homosexual persons are called to chastity. By the virtues of self-mastery that teach them inner freedom, at times by the support of disinterested friendship, by prayer and sacramental grace, they can and should gradually and resolutely approach Christian perfection."[17]

The catechism is saying to homosexuals: By turning to self-mastery, friendship, prayer, and the sacraments, you can escape the quagmire of homosexuality and gradually attain celibate Christian perfection. I suspect many homosexuals find this modus operandi curious and unrealistic. The catechism also advises homosexuals to unite their homosexuality "to the sacrifice of the Lord's Cross" but does not explain how this can be done.

The debate goes on. Is homosexuality caused by nature or by nurture or by free will? Is homosexuality biologically based or is it culturally determined or is it a chosen lifestyle? Are there other determining factors (besides nature and nurture) not yet recognized or understood? Maybe nature and nurture both play a role in molding homosexuals. And maybe Paul Abramson and Steven Pinkerton, the authors of *With Pleasure: Thoughts on the Nature of Human Sexuality*, are right in contending that the factors that determine a person's sexual proclivity "will forever remain a mystery."[18]

The Bible and Cultural Relativism

The moment has arrived, I am contending, when homosexuals should be delivered from the condemnatory jowls of the Jerry Falwells. Or to express the matter another way, homosexuals deserve to be rescued from self-righteous, acerbic Christians who throw moral stones at them. I am not suggesting that all Christians are condemnatory of homosexuals, but many are. Christians who persecute gays and lesbians have (unfortunately) a Damascus-road complex. Just as Paul—while traveling the road to Damascus so that he could persecute Christians found there—thought he was doing the right thing, similarly, Christians who persecute homosexuals think they are doing the right thing. They reason like this: Because the Bible condemns homosexuality, we—being Bible believers—condemn homosexuality. In other words, "We believe in going with the Bible." But this line of reasoning is not sound. *A moral norm or pronouncement is not necessarily true simply because that norm or pronouncement appears in the Bible.* Some moral views expressed in the Bible are obnoxious. No clear-thinking person in our time would accept them. Such is the case because biblical authors lived within culturally determined conceptual horizons that make some of their moral views obsolete.

Take, for example, the biblical attitude toward human slavery. In the ancient world slavery was as common as water in the ocean and darkness at night. Slave masters owned slaves and viewed them as property. Yet no sensitive person in our day believes that one person has a legal or moral right to own a fellow human being. All of us deem slavery, an inhumane relationship, to be morally repulsive. Yet the Bible takes human slavery for granted. This fact is disguised in English translations of the Bible, which refer to slaves with such euphemisms as "man-servant" and "maid-servant." Nowhere in biblical literature is slavery explicitly condemned. Instead, the Bible contains passages such as Lev 25:44–46, which asserts:

> As for the male and female slaves whom you may have, it is from the nations around you that you may acquire male and female slaves. You may also acquire them from among the aliens residing with you and from their families that are with you, who have been born in your land; and they may be your property. You may keep them as a possession for your children after you, for them to inherit as a property.

In Exod 21:20–21, a slave is recognized as being his master's property. This passage reads: "When a slaveowner strikes a male or female slave with a rod and the slave dies immediately, the owner shall be punished. But if the slave survives a day or two, there is no punishment; for the slave is the owner's property."

The law of Moses contains detailed slave legislation dealing with such matters as drilling a hole through a slave's ear (Exod 21:6), selling a daughter into slavery (Exod 21:7), and knocking out a slave's eye or tooth (Exod 21:26–27). Ephesians in the New Testament spells out guidelines for proper slave behavior (Eph 6:5–8). The letter to Philemon (also in the New Testament) concerns Onesimus, a runaway slave sent back to his owner by Saint Paul. Indeed, the Bible carries the institution of slavery all the way back to Noah (Gen 9:26–27).

Thus we confront the insight: On the issue of human slavery the Bible is a product of the era wherein it was written. It is historically conditioned. Slavery was an entrenched institution in the ancient Middle East and in the Roman Empire. The Old Testament, written against a Middle Eastern background, and the New Testament, composed in the context of the Roman Empire, presuppose human slavery. The biblical acceptance of slavery, an obnoxious institution, is an example of cultural relativism—the sociological theory that what we believe regarding various issues is at times molded by the cultural-historical setting in which we live. Our views are "time-conditioned." No person lives thousands of years ahead of his era.

Human slavery, however, is merely one example of the Bible's entrapment by cultural relativism and its containment of moral norms now viewed with disfavor. Deuteronomy 20:13 provides for the annihilation of male war prisoners. Is the slaughtering of war captives a practice that is morally acceptable? Should an unengaged woman marry a man who rapes her—provided her father has been paid fifty pieces of silver (as Deut 22:28–29 commands)?

The Old Testament book of Joshua is a war document containing an account of the Jewish conquest of Canaan (the promised land) in the 1200s B.C.E. This war document informs us that God ordered the mass extermination of the Canaanites. For example, Josh 11:19–20 asserts,

> There was not a town that made peace with the Israelites, except the Hivites, the inhabitants of Gibeon; all were taken in battle. For it was the Lord's doing to harden their hearts so that they would come against Israel in battle, in order that they might be utterly destroyed, and might receive no mercy, but be exterminated, just as the Lord had commanded Moses.

Can moral approval be given today to the commanding of a pogrom against the Canaanites? Can Christians or Jews take pride in the fact that the book of Joshua contains one of history's earliest accounts of a human holocaust? To express the issue another way, do contemporary Christians approve of genocide? I don't think so.

For emphasis, I repeat: *A moral norm or pronouncement is not necessarily true simply because that norm or pronouncement appears in the Bible.* I think this insight must be taken into account in evaluating the Bible's anti-homosexual pronouncements. For example, Lev 18:22 contains the anti-homosexual pronouncement: "You shall not lie with a male as with a woman; it is an abomination." But this same book of Leviticus also condemns eating lobsters, shrimp, ham sandwiches, and filet mignon cooked rare (Lev 11:1–10 and 19:26). Is Leviticus's condemnation of eating lobsters valid? Is its condemnation of homosexual behavior valid? Is homosexual behavior ipso facto morally reprehensible? If so, *why*? I have encountered moralists who contend that homosexual behavior is wrong. But we encounter again the disapproval dilemma. What is the precise dimension or the specific aspect of homosexual behavior that makes that behavior an abomination? I know of no moralist who has cogently or satisfactorily answered that question. Moreover, when the biblical authors of thousands of years ago condemned homosexuality, did they know about genetic programming? Did they know about societal conditioning? I doubt if they did. And I broach again the harm principle. If two homosexuals—preferably in private—express affection for one another, what harm are they doing to others? Do Christian moralists have a right or an obligation to pry into the private lives of homosexuals to discover *what* they are doing with *which* parts of their bodies? Who granted to Christian moralists dominion over homosexual behavior? Parenthetically, homosexuals express affection for one another in much the same way heterosexuals do.

An Appeal to Jerry Falwell

An appeal to Jerry Falwell from an imaginary homosexual:

> Dear Reverend Falwell,
> In our country you are a high-profile leader of fundamentalist Protestantism. I have seen you on television time and time again. On more than one occasion you have expressed negative feelings about those of us who are homosexual. You went so far as to accuse us of being partially responsible for the World Trade Center attacks of September 11, 2001. Please allow me to share one or two thoughts with you.
> First, many of us who are homosexual did not ask to be gays or lesbians. As far as our sexual orientation is concerned, we contend that we were born the way we are. Our innate sexual

orientation broaches questions I feel you have never confronted. One question concerns the sinfulness of homosexuality. Sinfulness, I'm sure you would agree, involves a deliberate choice by a rebellious will. But if we gays and lesbians did not rebelliously choose to be homosexual, then how can our unsought homosexuality be viewed by someone like you as being sinful? You ignore the dictum: no rebellious choice, no sin. Another question you do not confront concerns God. Who made us the way we are? Many of us who are homosexuals contend that God— the Heavenly Father of Christian tradition—formed us. In other words, we are God's creation. We feel God understands our condition and loves us as we are. If God loves us because he made us, why can't you—a minister of the gospel—love us also? Why do you despise us and label as vile those of us who are a part of God's creation?

If you wish to argue that we are not God's creation, then— pray tell—who created us the way we are and brought us into being? You may believe homosexuals have been created by a demonic force or by some inferior deity. What evidence do you have for this view? I know of none.

Additionally, are you aware that your condemnatory attitude (shared by scores of persons in the clergy) hurts us psychologically and has afflicted those of us who are homosexuals with devastating feelings of guilt and self-hate? Are you aware—and do you care—that your condemnatory attitude has alienated gays and lesbians from the church and from Christianity? Why go to church on Sunday when you know there's the possibility of being verbally assaulted by the person standing behind the pulpit? Why are so many members of the clergy—along with their parishioners—void of compassion and lacking in empathy for us? Those questions perplex me.

I suggest you take the time to read E. M. Forster's novel *Maurice*. One of the characters in this novel is named Clive, who is a homosexual. As a youngster Clive was deeply religious. He had a strong desire to reach out to God and to please him. But Clive believed he was damned because he had the impulse that destroyed the city of Sodom. Why had he out of all Christians been punished with a Sodomite inclination? In answer to these questions, Clive concluded that he was obliged to reject Christianity. As Forster observed, "Those who base their conduct upon what they are rather than upon what they ought to be" must always throw Christianity away. Writing in the same vein, Forster placed on the lips of one of the novel's characters (Lasker Jones) the observation, "England has always been disinclined to accept human nature."[19] I suggest, Reverend Falwell, that these words spoken about England could also be spoken about you. You are disinclined to accept human nature as it is. That is a mistake. It is a tragedy. I agree with the philosopher William Barrett, who contended that a person is bound to make a "sorry mess" of his life if he strives to live by what is for him an impossible-to-achieve moral code.[20]

Where does all this leave me? I must agree with Clive. Those of us who are homosexuals have no choice but to reject bureaucratic Christianity with its trappings of altars, creeds, stained glass windows, pompous pulpits, and incense pots. But this does not mean we are rejecting Jesus of Nazareth—a man described in the Gospels as "a glutton and a drunkard, a friend of tax collectors and sinners!" (Matt 11:19). Because Jesus associated with the scorned and the outcast, I feel he understands us. And I believe God understands us also. As I've said before, we are his handiwork.

An Appeal to Homosexuals

An appeal to homosexuals from an empathic heterosexual:

I want to share with you one or two thoughts. Make no mistake about it: The last half century has witnessed profound changes in

the attitude most of us in this country have about homosexuality.
For one thing, we have become aware of your existence. When
I was a youngster I didn't know homosexuals existed. I was an
adult before I became aware that there were gays and lesbians.
My awareness is due to your decision to "come out of the closet."
And my awareness is due to what is called the Gay Liberation
movement, which began, as some of you may not know, on a late
June night in 1969, when the police in New York City made what
started out to be a routine vice raid on the Stonewall Inn, a gay
bar in Greenwich Village. Officers released the bar's customers
one by one to the street to wait for transportation to the police
station. A crowd of homosexuals gathered to watch. And then the
unexpected happened. An arrested lesbian began fighting with
the police. The gathered crowd turned on the police and chaos
followed. Finding themselves assaulted by the outraged mob,
the police retreated and locked themselves inside the bar, which
someone then set fire to. Reinforcements arrived in time to rescue
the policemen trapped inside the burning bar. The riot that followed lasted far into the night. The next night saw more rioting.
Hundreds of police officers ended up battling thousands of homosexuals. On those two nights in late June of 1969, the Gay Liberation movement was born. Police raids on gay bars in Greenwich
Village ceased. And since the Stonewall Inn riots, the homosexual
community has become more and more high profile.

In fact, many of you who are gay or lesbian now flaunt your
sexual orientation as though it were a fashion statement. As you
ostentatiously display your sexual identity, please understand
that some of us who are heterosexual find it difficult—if not
impossible—to understand you. To us homosexuality is an
anthropological puzzle, a human enigma. Not wanting to sound
moralistic, I confess I have never experienced an erotic attraction toward a person of my own sex. Indeed, I cannot imagine
such. Thus we "straights" find homoerotic impulses perplexing
and we ask you to be understanding of our perplexity.

Moreover, have you pondered the possibility that the extravagant flaunting of your sexual orientation is counterproductive? That it is aesthetically repulsive, leaving a bad taste in the mouths of some people? My judgment in this regard is aesthetic, not moral. For example, I wish gay or heterosexual couples would not hug, kiss, and fondle one another extravagantly while walking about San Francisco. And what about gay pride parades? I have seen more than one. Participants in gay pride parades—by their bizarre dress and antics—make themselves look silly.

I suggest that the Gay Liberation movement has done as much as anything else to stimulate the prurient, voyeuristic tendency of this country's media. Today's media revels in trumpeting as loudly as possible the sexual "indiscretions" of prominent people. This has not always been the case. Simply compare the way the press dealt with Franklin Delano Roosevelt's longtime liaison with Lucy Rutherford and Bill Clinton's liaison with Monica Lewinsky.

So my unsought advice to you is: *cool it!* And bear in mind that scores of us who are heterosexual wish those of you who are homosexual nothing but the best. We have this wish for you although we do not understand you.

Two Suggestions

Some epochs in human history are stagnant in that events move slowly. Others are transitional, characterized by rapid change. The eighteenth century, with the American and French Revolutions and with a revolt against the theory of the divine right of kings, was such a transitional epoch. Similarly, the church—now two thousand years old—has experienced transitional epochs. The sixteenth century, with its emergence of Protestantism, was a transitional period. The church is now being forced to pass through yet another transitional era as far as homosexuality is concerned. For centuries the church taught that homosexuals were hardened sinners destined for hell. Moreover, the subject was taboo: "Nice people don't talk about homosexuality." But today people are as aware of homosexuality as they are of heterosexuality.

Thus a question emerges: Where should the church, experiencing moral vertigo in this transitional era, go from here in its attitude toward and in its teachings about homosexuality? Transitional periods are always characterized by doubt, confusion, and lack of certainty. Recognizing these characteristics, I want now to emphasize two ideas I have briefly mentioned previously.

First, I suggest that the church should confess that its past draconian condemnation of homosexuality was wrong. Homosexuals are children of God. When one inquires, one discovers that practically every family is touched by homosexuality in the sense that an uncle or an aunt or a cousin or a nephew or a sibling is homosexual. For the church to teach that these beloved relatives are perverts destined for hell is as atrocious as it is insensitive. To use a biblical term, the church should repent. The literal meaning of the New Testament term for repentance (*metanoia*) is "a change of mind." The church should change its mind on the issue of homosexuality—replacing condemnation with sympathy and understanding.

Second, I think the homosexual community should give Christian heterosexuals time to mentally digest and assimilate a changed attitude toward homosexuality. To that end I think a "low profile" strategy by homosexuals is in order. Recently Episcopalians in New Hampshire saw fit to choose Gene Robinson, a homosexual priest, for their bishop. Having divorced his wife, the Reverend Robinson had been living openly with a male companion for years. Suppose this priest—instead of living with a male lover—had been living for years with a woman to whom he was not married. Would the Episcopalians of New Hampshire have chosen him to be their bishop? I doubt it. Maybe they were trying to be avant-garde. The ordination of Gene Robinson as bishop of New Hampshire has caused no small amount of controversy and distress within the Episcopal Church. I think it would have been better for Gene Robinson to have maintained a low profile and not to have allowed himself to be elevated to the status of bishop. In this regard I think the words of Saint Paul are relevant: "Therefore, if food is a cause of their falling, I will never eat meat, so that I may not cause one of them to fall" (1 Cor 8:13). Paul wrote these words centuries ago to Christians living in the city of Corinth. Some Corinthian Christians were troubled that fellow believers were eating meat that had been butchered in pagan temples, which were the meat markets of the Mediterranean world of two thousand years ago. They believed that this meat was permeated with the presence or power of pagan gods. If believers ate this meat they ran the danger of having the power of pagan gods within them (this belief is responsible for the word enthusiasm— literally, "god inside you"). Paul knew such meat was not permeated with the power of pagan gods. Yet out of concern for fellow believers who held such a belief he asserted: "If food is a cause of their falling, I will never eat meat." I think this concern for the feelings of others is relevant to the current homosexual controversy. Homosexuals should say, "If others find my sexual orientation puzzling or troubling, I will not flaunt my sexual orientation before them."

NOTES

1. T. G. Johnson, *Sappho the Lesbian* (London: Williams & Norgate, 1899).

2. *Philo*, trans. F. H. Colson, Loeb Classical Library (Cambridge, Mass., 1959), 6:69–71.

3. Josephus, *Antiquities of the Jews* (Philadelphia: John C. Winston Company, 1809), 47.

4. Augustine, *City of God*, XVI, 30. Quotations from *City of God* are taken mainly from R. W. Dyson, *The City of God against the Pagans* (New York: Cambridge University Press, 2001).

5. *Fleta*, trans. H. G. Richardson and G. O. Sayles (London: Bernard Quaritech, 1955), 2:3.

6. *Britton*, trans. Francis Morgan Nichols (Washington, D.C.: John Byrne & Company, 1901), 1:3

7. This quotation from Blackstone's *Commentaries on the Laws of England* appears in Derrick Bailey, *Homosexuality and the Western Christian Tradition* (London: Longmans, Green, & Company, 1955), 153.

8. The "sin" or "immoral" or "illegal" conception of same-sex sexual activity dominated the colonies and the United States before the late nineteenth century. During this era the modern concept of homosexuality did not exist. Hence law codes condemned same-sex sexual conduct. See Irving Sloan, *Homosexual Conduct and the Law* (London: Oceana Publications, 1987), 89. See Arthur S. Leonard, *Homosexual Conduct and State Regulation* (New York: Garland Publishing, 1997), ix, 15–16, 20, 51. See Editors of the Harvard Law Review, *Sexual Orientation and the Law* (Cambridge: Harvard University Press, 1989), 2–4. The negative attitude of the Plymouth Colony and the Massachusetts Bay Colony toward homosexuality can also be found on pages 47 to 53 of William B. Rubenstein, *Lesbians, Gay Men, and the Law* (New York: The New Press, 1993).

9. Parenthetically, a virulent homophobia is rampant today among African Americans. Alan Keyes, a black politician, has asserted that homosexuals have chosen a lifestyle based "simply on the premise of selfish hedonism."

10. Francis Mark Mondimore, "Homosexuality," *Encyclopedia Americana* (Danbury: Scholastic Library Publishing, Inc., 2004), 14:333–35.

11. Paul Abramson and Steven Pinkerton, *With Pleasure: Thoughts on the Nature of Human Sexuality* (Oxford: Oxford University Press, 2002), 13.

12. Ibid., 97–98, 136–37.

13. Francis Mark Mondimore, *A Natural History of Homosexuality* (Baltimore: Johns Hopkins University Press, 1996).

14. E. M. Forster, *Maurice* (New York: W. W. Norton & Company, 1971), 69.

15. *Catechism of the Catholic Church* (Liguori, Mo.: Liguori Publications, 1994), 566, paragraph 2357.

16. *Los Angeles Times*, September 20, 2001, B3.

17. *Catechism of the Catholic Church*, 566, paragraph 2359.

18. Abramson and Pinkerton, *With Pleasure*, 137.

19. Forster, *Maurice*, 211.

20. William Barrett, *Irrational Man* (New York: Doubleday Anchor Books, 1958), 170.

Fornication, Adultery, and the Harm Principle

A Definition of Terms

When writing on a topic (in this case the controversial topics of forni-cation and adultery), an author should have in mind the audience—the readership—he is targeting. Authors cannot expect what they write to interest or to apply to everyone. In light of this insight, I want to clar-ify for whom I wrote the discussion that immediately follows. What audience am I targeting? I am not writing for high school students who have Saturday-night sexual trysts (and who have no hesitancy about conceiving babies out of wedlock—babies they expect society to sup-port financially through this country's welfare system). I am not writ-ing for college students who have fraternity beer-and-sex parties. Neither am I targeting men and women who appear in salacious pho-tographs on the pages of slick girlie magazines. Nor am I writing for those pathetic souls who appear on television programs such as Howard Stern's. The behavior of persons in these non-targeted cate-gories confirms the Samuel Purchas proverb: *corruptio optima pessima*, "The best things corrupted become the worst." Nor am I writing for secularists who have no interest in ethics or religion. Instead, I am writing for men and women in their late twenties and beyond who are single, widowed, or divorced and who have been socialized into the church's sexual morality and, consequently, have had their beliefs about sexual behavior molded (or twisted) by puritanical moral dictators who speak in the name of the church. I am also writing for husbands and wives trapped in fatigued marriages. Some marriages are like automobile tires or shoe soles; with the passing of time they become frayed and wear out. In other words, I have in mind mature men and women who are morally sensitive and want to do the "right thing" as far as their sexual conduct is concerned.

A definition of terms is in order. I suggest we give attention first to adultery. In grappling with this term I want us to observe in particular that the church's understanding of adultery is not the same as the biblical understanding of adultery. This point cannot be emphasized too strongly. In biblical thought adultery refers to voluntary intercourse between a married woman and a man other than her husband. In other words, adultery is copulation with a married woman. There is no biblical law against extramarital intercourse on the part of a married man. An article on adultery in the *Encyclopedia Judaica* bears this out: "The extramarital intercourse of a married man is not *per se* a crime in biblical or later Jewish law."[1] In biblical jurisprudence a married man is allowed to have sexual intercourse with an unmarried woman. Consider King Solomon with his harem of hundreds of mistresses (concubines). It is not easy to convey to "Bible-rulebook" Christians the insight that biblical ethics do not prohibit extramarital intercourse on the part of married men. They have been conditioned to believe that the Bible teaches that it is sinful or immoral for a married man to copulate with any woman other than his wife.

Ignoring the biblical definition of adultery, the church defines adultery as *all instances* of extramarital sexual intercourse. Adultery is committed if a married man copulates with any woman other than his wife. Adultery is committed if a married woman copulates with any man other than her husband. "Adultery refers to marital infidelity. When two partners, of whom at least one is married to another party, have sexual relations—even transient ones—they commit adultery."[2] Thus affirms the catechism of the Roman Catholic Church. Grassroots Protestantism agrees with this definition. In defining adultery the church is like Lewis Carroll's Humpty Dumpty, who said, "When I use a word it means just what I choose it to mean—neither more nor less."

Adultery is forbidden in the seventh commandment of the Decalogue while the tenth prohibits the desire for another man's wife (Exod 20:14, 17; Deut 5:18, 21). Biblical law states that both parties in adultery should be put to death (Lev 20:13; Deut 22:22).

What is the specific aspect of adultery that makes it an abomination? Curiously, the Bible never explicitly states *why* adultery is wrong, although theories abound concerning why it was frowned upon. One theory: in biblical thought a wife was viewed as a husband's property; thus to copulate with a married woman was a violation of her husband's property rights. Another theory: sexual exclusivity assured clear paternity. And another theory: the prohibition of adultery prevented a married woman from developing bonds that could weaken the family unit. Theories aside, why the Bible condemns adultery remains a puzzle.

Having grappled with the term adultery, I want now to give attention to the word fornication. In English-language Bibles, "fornication" is used to translate the Greek word *porneia*. *Porneia* is related to the Greek word *porne*, which means "harlot." "Pornography" is derived from *porne* and literally means "writing about harlots." But the word *porneia*, alas, is an interpretive puzzle. At no place in the New Testament is the term explicitly defined. Repeatedly it is used in a general sense to designate any kind of sexual immorality. For example, in 1 Cor 5:1, fornication (*porneia*) refers to a member of the Corinthian church living with his father's wife. The term appears in Matt 5:32, where Jesus forbids divorce "except for *porneia*." What Jesus meant by this exception is not obvious. As best etymologists can tell, fornication was a broad term meaning sexual immorality or licentiousness. Roman Catholicism and conservative Protestantism, however, have given "fornication" a narrow or specific meaning, that is, to designate copulation between unmarried persons. They have constructed this definition in spite of the fact that neither in the Old Testament nor in the New Testament is there explicit condemnation of sexual intercourse between unmarried persons. Be that as it may, the current catechism of the Roman Catholic Church asserts: "*Fornication* is carnal union between an unmarried man and an unmarried woman. It is gravely contrary to the dignity of persons and of human sexuality which is naturally ordered to the good of spouses and the generation and education of children."[3] In defining fornication the church again is like Humpty Dumpty: "When I use a word it means just what I choose it to mean—neither more nor less."

The Sinfulness of Fornication

I want us now to confront two questions. Is fornication (copulation between unmarried persons) wrong or sinful? And is adultery (marital infidelity) wrong or sinful?

I deal first with fornication. In doing so allow me to construct the following scenario. Frances, a high school math teacher, is a forty-eight-year-old widow whose husband was killed in an automobile accident. She is also the mother of four daughters, all of whom are teenagers. One day by chance—while grocery shopping—she meets a man named Fred. Fred, a real estate salesman by profession, is a fifty-year-old widower whose wife died of cancer. He is also the father of three children—two sons and a mentally incapacitated daughter who is confined to a wheelchair. Over time Frances and Fred, both of whom have heavy familial responsibilities, develop a friendship that evolves into one of great depth. Both are a ray of love and light and a source of adult companionship in each other's lives. Yet both recognize that marriage would present all kinds of difficulties, some familial, some legal, some emotional. What man is eager to assume financial responsibility for four stepdaughters? What woman is eager to assume responsibility for a mentally incapacitated stepdaughter? Yet Fred and Frances, both lonely, care for one another, enjoy each other's company, and are sexually attracted to one another. On a weekend in August—after a year of companionship—they check into a Hilton Hotel and engage in consensual sexual intercourse. This they have done several times since.

The conduct of Frances and Fred broaches questions. Are they fornicators? The church would answer: Yes! Are Frances and Fred guilty of committing sexual acts that are wrong and sinful? Again the church would answer: Yes! The church would answer this way because it has subjected human sexuality to what can be labeled maritalization confinement. I am referring to the church's view that marriage is the *only context* within which a man and a woman can rightfully engage in sexual intercourse. Because of this maritalization confinement, our language abounds with such expressions as premarital sex, marital sex, and extramarital sex. Maritalization confinement explains why youngsters raised within conservative religious families (both Catholic and Protestant) unwisely marry at a very early age. They marry early so they can have sex.

But issues arise that the church tends to ignore. There is what I am calling the disapproval dilemma. To be sure, Fred and Frances copulated. But why does the church disapprove of their copulation? What, pray tell, is the precise dimension or aspect of their sexual liaison that makes the liaison sinful or wrong? What's the problem? Moreover, still thinking in a casuistic manner, should not their liaison be judged in light of the harm principle (meaning that the only circumstance under which society or the church has a right to condemn and to prohibit a given sexual behavior is to prevent a person from doing harm to others)? What harm did Frances and Fred do to others by engaging in a discreet consensual sexual relationship? I can think of none. Why does the church become so upset if two lonely people express affection for one another? Why does the church become agitated if two unmarried people enjoy sexual pleasure? And why does the church and society—at least in some quarters—continue to have a gloomy *Scarlet Letter* hangover? I can think of scores of situations in which widows, widowers, the divorced, and folk who never married would have their lives enriched by receiving tender physical affection from a person of the opposite sex. Their lives would also be enriched by giving tender physical affection to someone of the opposite sex. Yet many refrain from doing so because they have been conditioned to believe they would be guilty of fornication. My conclusion (which you as a reader have every right to reject): There is nothing wrong or sinful about responsible unmarried men and women engaging in sexual relations. To label such sexual relations as fornication is as unwarranted as it is insulting.

Adultery and the Harm Principle

I now turn to the nettlesome issue of adultery. Examining this issue (about which people have strong feelings) is like walking into a hornet's nest. The following examination of adultery will contend that whereas masturbation, homosexuality, and fornication pass the harm test, adultery does not. It does not pass the harm test because of the extravagant "romantic" conception of marriage that is widespread today in Western society. Adultery—I shall soon explain—is commonly viewed as a violation of one's marriage or wedding vows.

The issues of adultery and marriage are intertwined. As previously observed, the church abandoned the biblical conception of adultery (copulation of a married woman with a man other than her husband) and adopted the expanded view that adultery is copulation between a husband and someone other than his wife or copulation between a wife and someone other than her husband. Thus adultery—so many Christians believe—is a violation of the Christian conception of marriage—a conception that prohibits all extramarital intercourse. Curiously, scores of people believe a static "Christian conception of marriage" has existed from Jesus' time all the way down to the present. This static conception, which exists in popular piety and which churches promulgate, has at least two core parts. One core part is monogamy (the state of being married to one person only). The second core part involves romance: "A man and woman marry because they love one another."

Why churches see fit to promulgate this two-part conception of marriage (monogamy and love intoxication) is puzzling. I say this because over the centuries different attitudes toward marriage have existed within Christendom. Evidence suggests that foundational personalities such as Jesus and Paul had a negative attitude toward sex and marriage. Indeed, the original Christian ideal for sex and marriage was of a "new and spiritual life" that transcended sex and marriage. Consider Jesus' example and words. Jesus, unlike the Buddha or Moses or Mohammed, was not married. He evidently had a jaundiced view of marriage because he rejected the idea of marriage in a future life. This rejection came in the context of an attempt by Sadducees to befuddle Jesus on the issue of marriage.

> Some Sadducees, who say that there is no resurrection, came to him and asked him a question, saying, "Teacher, Moses wrote for us that if a man's brother dies, leaving a wife but no child, the man shall marry the widow and raise up children for his brother. There were seven brothers; the first married and, when he died, left no children; and the second married the widow and died, leaving no children; and the third likewise; none of the seven left children. Last of all, the woman herself died. In the resurrection whose wife will she be? For the seven had married her." Jesus said to them, "Is not this the reason you are wrong, that you know not neither the scriptures nor the power of God? For when they rise from the dead, they neither marry nor are given in marriage, but are like angels in heaven." (Mark 12:18–25)

Thus Jesus believed that marriages would not exist in the future world because people would be like sexless angels. The linking of celibacy and eternal life is found also in the Jesus statement recorded in Luke 20:34–36: "Those who belong to this age marry and are given in marriage; but those who are considered worthy of a place in that age and in the resurrection from the dead neither marry nor are given in marriage. Indeed they cannot die any more, because they are like angels and are children of God, being children of the resurrection." Thus, in Jesus' thought, marriage was a feature of "this age," but those who aspire to the resurrection from the dead, an existence superior to "this age," would not marry. This Jesus saying about "no marriage in heaven" is hardly a ringing endorsement of marriage on this earth.

There are occasions in which Jesus denigrated the traditional biological family and suggested it be replaced by a "family" consisting of his followers. Consider the episode recorded in Matt 12:46–50.

> While he was still speaking to the crowds, his mother and his brothers were standing outside, wanting to speak to him. Someone told him, "Look, your mother and your brothers are standing outside, wanting to speak to you." But to the one who had told him this, Jesus replied, "Who is my mother, and who are my brothers?" And pointing to his disciples, he said, "Here are my mother and my brothers! For whoever does the will of my Father in heaven is my brother and sister and mother."

Elsewhere Jesus taught that faithful discipleship provokes the rending of traditional biological families. Consider this Jesus quotation found in Matt 10:34–37.

> Do not think that I have come to bring peace to the earth; I have not come to bring peace, but a sword. For I have come to set a man against his father, and a daughter against her mother, and a daughter-in-law against her mother-in-law; and one's foes will be members of one's own household. Whoever loves father or mother more than me is not worthy of me; and whoever loves son or daughter more than me is not worthy of me.

Thus Jesus discipleship undercut family obligations and created intra-family conflicts. One man wanted to bury his father before following Jesus. Jesus' response was, "Let the dead bury their own dead; but as for you, go and proclaim the kingdom of God" (Luke 9:60). Peter poignantly remarked to Jesus, "Look, we have left our homes and followed you" (Luke 18:28). Jesus' riposte was, "Truly I tell you, there is no one who has left house or wife or brothers or parents or children, for the sake of the kingdom of God, who will not get back very much more in this age, and in the age to come eternal life" (Luke 18:29–30). This statement is draconian. "Abandon your family—and that includes children—for the sake of the kingdom of God." In its teachings, the contemporary church revels in clichés. One of those clichés is "Follow Jesus!" If following Jesus is the model or standard, it is difficult to see what the paradigm for Christian marriage and family should be.

Paul shared Jesus' point of view. His negative attitude toward sexuality and marriage is spelled out in his first letter to the Corinthian church.

> Now concerning the matters about which you wrote: "It is well for a man not to touch a woman." But because of cases of sexual immorality, each man should have his own wife and each woman her own husband. The husband should give to his wife her conjugal rights, and likewise the wife to her husband. For the wife does not have the authority over her own body, but the husband does; likewise the husband does not have authority over his own body, but the wife does. Do not deprive one another except perhaps by agreement for a set time, to devote yourselves to prayer, and then come together again, so that Satan may not tempt you because of your lack of self-control. This I say by way of concession, not of command. I wish that all were as I myself am. But each has his own particular gift from God, one having one kind and another a different kind. To the unmarried and the widows I say that it is well for them to remain unmarried as I am. But if they are not practicing self-control, they should marry. For it is better to marry than to be aflame with passion. (1 Cor 7:1–9)

This passage reveals that Paul

- believed that never touching a woman was a commendable practice ("It is well for a man not to touch a woman"),
- viewed marriage as a compromising solution to an intractable libido ("It is better to marry than to be aflame with passion"), and
- commended celibacy ("To the unmarried and the widows I say that it is well for them to remain unmarried as I am").

This applauding of celibacy and negativity toward marriage (an outlet for lust to be avoided if at all possible) passed over into the early church. Celibate ascetics—disdaining marriage—became the church's heroes and heroines. To the point is the observation of W. E. H. Lecky:

> If an impartial person were to glance over the ethics of the New Testament, and were asked, what was the central and distinctive virtue

to which the sacred writers most continually referred, he would doubt-less answer that it was that which is described as love, charity, or phi-lanthropy. If he were to apply a similar scrutiny to the writings of the fourth and fifth centuries, he would answer that the cardinal virtue of the religious type was not love, but chastity. And this chastity, which was regarded as the ideal state, was not the purity of an undefiled mar-riage. It was the absolute suppression of the whole sensual side of our nature. The chief form of virtue, the central conception of the saintly life, was a perpetual struggle against all carnal impulses, by men who altogether refused the compromise of marriage.[4]

Rejecting human sexuality and marriage, Christian celibate ascetics prided themselves on having tortured and filthy bodies. "Lice were called the pearls of God, and to be covered with them was an indispen-sable mark of a holy man."[5] "St. Marcarius of Alexandria slept in a marsh, and exposed his body naked to the stings of venomous flies."[6] Saint Abraham the hermit lived for fifty years after his conversion; dur-ing these five decades he refused to wash either his feet or his face (110). Silvia, a famous virgin, refused to wash any part of her body except her fingers (110). Saint Euphraxia joined a convent that had more than one hundred nuns; all of them shuddered at the mention of a bath (110). The celibate par excellence was an old-timer named Saint Simeon Stylites. "A horrible stench, intolerable to bystanders, exhaled from his body, and worms dropped from him whenever he moved" (112). Saint Simeon constructed a pillar (or platform) that was sixty feet tall. For thirty years he lived on top of this platform. For a whole year he stood on one leg, "the other being covered with hideous ulcers, while his biog-rapher was commissioned to stand by his side, to pick up the worms that fell from his body, and to replace them in the sores, the saint saying to the worm, 'Eat what God has given you'" (112).

Obviously celibates such as Saint Simeon (his body oozing worms) and Saint Macarius (his body assaulted by flies) did not possess a "Chris-tian conception of marriage." The question of how the church eventu-ally got around to hammering out a "Christian conception of marriage" is a question that is agonizingly complex. It is dealt with in great detail in a book entitled *From Sacrament to Contract* by John Witte Jr., who is the Jonas Robitscher Professor of Law and Ethics at Emory University in Atlanta. *From Sacrament to Contract* is an illuminating account of various understandings of marriage that have existed across the centuries within the church. According to Witte, the church did not develop "a systematic theology and law of marriage" until the late eleventh century through the thirteenth.[7] This marital theology and law took place in the wake of the papal revolution of Pope Gregory VII (1073–1085). The Roman Catholic Church came to perceive itself as an "autonomous legal and political corporation within Western Christendom" and in this capacity saw fit to view marriage as one of the seven sacraments.[8] The church did so by appealing to the Latin Vulgate's translation of Eph 5:23–33, in which the discussion of marriage and husband-wife relationships includes the following description: "This is a great sacrament"(Eph 5:32). On the basis of this Latin statement, Thomas Aquinas and other medieval thinkers elevated marriage to the status of a sacrament, along with baptism and the Eucharist. Unfortunately, the Latin word *sacramentum* in Eph 5:32 is a mistranslation of the Greek word *mysterion* (mystery). Thus the verse should be translated, "This is a great mystery" rather than "This is a great sacrament." Building beliefs on mistranslated Greek words, as Thomas Aquinas did, is not the wisest of theological procedures.

In contemporary Protestantism, marriage has undergone still another mutation. In Protestantism, marriages are predicated on romance (a motif that is lacking in Roman Catholic matrimonial liturgy). Weddings have become celebrations of human love. On occasion brides and grooms are allowed to construct their own wedding ceremonies. They embellish these ceremonies with maudlin love songs. These love songs affirm: "Every time our eyes meet, this feeling inside me is almost more than I can take. Baby when you touch me, I can feel how much you love me, and it just blows me away." These just-quoted words are from a wedding song entitled "Amazed." Religious bookstores sell books of wedding songs. For example, one of these is entitled *The Forever Mine Wedding Songbook*. Among its twenty wedding songs are "Can't Help Falling in Love," "Endless Love," "The

Power of Love," "When I Fall in Love," and "I Finally Found Someone." Another collection of wedding songs is entitled *Timeless Wedding Standards*. Among its thirty-eight wedding songs are "Baby, Come to Me," "I Only Have Eyes for You," "Let Me Call You Sweetheart," "Love and Marriage," "Saving All My Love for You," and "Love Will Keep Us Alive."

The standard Protestant wedding liturgy challenges grooms with such demands as: "Wilt thou have this woman to be thy wedded wife, to live together in the holy state of matrimony? Wilt thou love her, comfort her, honor and keep her, in sickness and in health; and forsaking all others keep thee only unto her so long as ye both shall live?" The liturgy continues: "I take thee to be my wedded wife, to have and to hold from this day forward, for better, for worse, for richer, for poorer, in sickness and in health, to love and to cherish, until death us do part." Similar demands are made of the bride.

Witness the appeal to love ("wilt thou love her") and to exclusivity ("forsaking all others keep thee only unto her"). And witness the time span involved ("until death us do part"). Thus a bride and groom (both frequently in their late teens or early twenties) vow to live together in an exclusive monogamous relationship for the rest of their lives. These are heavy demands, which can burden any marriage with an expectation overload. According to the 2000 federal census, the median age for males marrying is 26.8 years and the median age for women marrying is 25.1 years. Yet thousands of couples marry younger than these ages.[9]

But in the course of a wedding service this expectation overload is ignored. Instead, at the ceremony's conclusion the minister presiding will say to the newly minted husband: "You may now kiss your wife." These words about kissing reflect the romantic nature of wedding ceremonies. While the newly minted husband kisses his just-acquired wife, the congregation in attendance giggles and applauds. The connection between Jesus, the crucified Jew, and a kissing couple (the husband in a tuxedo, the wife in a long-flowing wedding gown) is not obvious. Wedding ceremonies and marriage vows, it must be conceded, are constructs of the church. Whether these constructs are rational is another issue.

The marinating of marriage in from-the-wedding-altar-to-the-grave romance explains why adultery does not pass the harm test. Newly married couples assume that their love intoxication will last forever and will never attenuate. And they assume that their mutual sexual attraction will never diminish. They are blissfully unaware that they are being foxed or conned by Mother Nature. The human race must be perpetuated. To that end Mother Nature instills within young pubertal men and women an intense sexual desire: "More than anything else, I want to have sex!" They capitulate to this intense sexual desire, get married, and have children. Thereby they fulfill the quip: "First comes love, then comes marriage, then comes Mary with a baby carriage." And so the human race is perpetuated from one generation to another. Apart from the stimulus of intense sexual desire I doubt if men and women would bother to assume the burdens and responsibilities of marriage and parenthood.

Thus couples enter marriage assuming they have a lifetime of perpetually satisfying romantic monopoly on one another. But alas! After ten or twenty years of married life the unanticipated happens. The romantic fire begins to flicker. The mutual sexual attraction begins to lessen. The husband and wife develop different interests and grow apart. Familiarity breeds—if not contempt—dissatisfaction. In the context of this marital ennui it is easy for a husband or a wife to develop an interest in someone else and commit adultery. If the spouse doesn't find out, the adulterous episode silently glides by—sailing away like a ship putting out to sea. But alas again! On occasion the husband or wife finds out. An anger explosion follows. Most of the time this anger explosion is not moral in nature. The wife does not say to her husband, "You are an immoral person! You violated the seventh commandment!" Nor does the husband say to the wife, "You are an immoral person! You violated the seventh commandment!" Instead of moral anger, post-adultery anger explosions are usually emotional or psychological by nature: "You bastard, you cheated on me!" Or, "You bitch, you cheated on me!" The husband or wife continues: "You've been untrue! I feel betrayed! You violated our marriage vows!" Permeating these anger

97

explosions are feelings of fear, jealousy, insecurity, and rejection: "My wife no longer finds me sexually attractive"; "My husband no longer loves me as he once did." I can understand a husband reasoning as follows: "My wife cheated on me and I feel like a fool. I'm the community cuckold." And I can understand a wife reasoning as follows: "I've invested my life in my husband, my home, and my children. I spent all my time, effort, and energy to create a secure and comfortable life for us all, only to find out that he has been fooling around. My once secure world is falling apart." I shall never forget one of my acquaintances remarking, "Women in particular are 'nesters.' They don't want anything to happen to their nest."

On occasion a "betrayed" husband or a "betrayed" wife reacts hysterically, having an anger orgy and becoming violent. The Clara and David Harris tragedy is a classic example of a wife reacting with jealous rage over a husband's infidelity. Clara and David Harris, both forty-four years old, both dentists, both millionaires, were married on Valentine's Day in 1992. They ran a jointly owned corporation that operated six dental offices in the Houston, Texas, area. David Harris was a courteous and suave man who loved music. Shortly before his death he had purchased a $90,000 Steinway piano. He became involved in an extramarital affair with Gail Bridges, a divorced mother of three who worked as his office receptionist. On July 24, 2002, David Harris and Gail Bridges had a romantic tryst at the Nassau Bay Hilton Inn located close to the Johnson Space Center. While leaving the Hilton Inn together they were confronted in the lobby by Clara Harris, David Harris's wife. An altercation followed. As David Harris left the Hilton, his livid wife followed him to the hotel's parking lot, got into her Mercedes, and killed him by running over him three times. Witnesses stated that the first time Clara Harris hit her husband he was propelled more than ten feet into the air. She left her husband pinned under a front tire of her gray Mercedes. An autopsy revealed that he had sixteen broken ribs, as well as a broken jaw, back, pelvis, and collarbone. Moreover, his lungs were punctured. As a bizarre footnote, this assault was witnessed by David Harris's sixteen-year-old daughter from a previous marriage who was riding as a passenger in the Mercedes with her stepmother. Whether Clara Harris was justified in murdering her husband is beside the point. What I am belaboring is that this Houston tragedy—and it was a tragedy—illustrates the outrage and the hurt a person can experience on discovering that his or her spouse is engaged in an extramarital affair. During the altercation in the Hilton lobby Clara Harris screamed at Gail Bridges, "You bitch! He's my husband!" And so I repeat: *adultery does not pass the harm test*.[10] The Harris tragedy brings into focus the hyperpossessiveness some people have toward their spouses.

Parenthetically, the extravagant attention given in the media to this Houston episode (which has come to be known as the "Mercedes murder") illustrates a sad feature of contemporary American society that I have already noted: the prurient, voyeuristic interest of the media in sexual indiscretions. Schopenhauer condemned *Schadenfreude* in section 114 of chapter VIII in volume II of his *Parerge and Paralipomena*. He wrote as follows: "But it is Schadenfreude, a mischievous delight in the misfortunes of others, which remains the worst trait in human nature. It is a feeling which is closely akin to cruelty, and differs from it, to say the truth, only as theory from practice." Void of compassion, this country's media (unintentionally revealing a Puritan hangover) rejoice in *Schadenfreude* when it comes to sexual indiscretions. They revel in the scandalous and view the humiliation of people as sport.

Ponder what the media did to Bill Clinton. Reporters became peeping-tom sex police and tried to transform Clinton's private missteps with Monica Lewinsky into the legacy of his presidency.

Consider what the media did to Gary Hart. For a time Gary Hart was a U.S. senator from Colorado. A brilliant man, he had once contemplated being a minister, even studying at the Yale Divinity School. While at Yale he transferred to its law school and graduated with a degree in law. As a congressman he was a member of the Armed Services Committee and chaired a subcommittee on nuclear power. In 1984, he ran unsuccessfully for the Democratic presidential nomination. During the campaign, the nation's media had a holiday disclosing his extramarital improprieties. From one end of the country to the other they plastered pictures of Hart sitting in front of a yacht named *Monkey Business* with a woman other than his wife sitting on his lap.

Ponder too what the media did to the late Wilbur Mills, an Arkansas congressman. Mills, a Democrat, was elected to the U.S. House of Representatives in 1938, and served there until 1977. Chairman of the Ways and Means Committee, Mills became known in the early 1970s as the most powerful person in Congress. The nation's media had a fine time reporting that he was linked romantically to Fannie Foxe, an Argentine striptease dancer. She is gleefully remembered in the media for jumping one night out of Wilbur Mills's limousine and leaping fully clothed into a reflection pool on the Washington Mall.

Having acknowledged that adultery does not pass the harm test, I now broach the question: Is Western society's attitude toward extramarital affairs realistic? Has a moment arrived when society and the church need to rethink their hot-as-Tabasco-sauce, wholesale disapproval of extramarital affairs? Momentarily I shall discuss factors—such as longevity—that encourage extramarital affairs because they contribute to the expectation overload some marriages experience. Before discussing those factors, however, I want to congratulate husbands and wives who remain "true" to one another. Scores of husbands and wives live out their adult years in a satisfying monogamous relationship; "they have eyes only for one another." Such a lifelong loving companionship is beautiful and should be held in esteem.

Yet this commendable, we-have-eyes-only-for-one-another relationship is not followed by all husbands and wives. Honesty compels the admission that some husbands and wives engage in extramarital affairs. Are all of these affairs morally reprehensible? Should all of them be condemned? Are there mitigating circumstances? Suppose a husband is married to an invalid, semi-paralyzed wife who must live permanently in a nursing home. Imagine a wife whose catatonic-schizophrenic husband has been committed to a mental hospital. Visualize a husband whose wife—because of puritanical religious scruples—is frigid as far as sexual loving is concerned, with her thinking that "nice girls don't go in for that stuff." Consider a wife whose husband has come down with Alzheimer's disease or a husband whose wife cares nothing about her physical appearance, never exercising, possessing putrid tobacco breath, becoming excessively corpulent, and the like. Should spouses entangled in these situations be condemned if they stray from the straight and narrow? Are not all of these but unfortunate circumstances that people stumble into—or have thrust upon them—while experiencing the imperfect condition known as human existence?

Moreover, there are factors that the church ignores but which make a lifelong monogamous relationship problematic. I shall discuss two: longevity and the biological desire (or imperative) for sexual variety. In discussing these factors (the second of which can be labeled the "Jimmy Carter" factor), I am not attempting to justify extramarital affairs. But I am seeking to understand them. And I am also pleading for compassion (rather than hot coals of condemnation) for husbands and wives who stray from the straight and narrow.

First, the longevity factor. To state the obvious: people live longer than they once did. Consequently, marriages last longer than they once did. Back in colonial days American marriages probably lasted less than a dozen years.[11] Now "until death do us part" can mean a commitment of forty to fifty to sixty years or more. For a husband and a wife to maintain an intense romantic relationship for over a half century is difficult. To be sure, at the beginning of a marriage the romantic-sexual attraction between a husband and a wife is intense. This intensity is recognized in the Bible wherein newly married men were not expected to fulfill military duties. Deuteronomy 24:5 asserts: "When a man is newly married, he shall not go out with the army or be charged with any related duty. He shall be free at home one year, to be happy with the wife whom he has married." Proverbs 5:18–19 (quoting ex parte) asserts: "Rejoice in the wife of your youth. . . . May her breasts satisfy you at all times; may you be intoxicated always by her love."

But is perpetual love intoxication between a husband and a wife psychologically possible? I have alluded to this problem previously. I wish now to emphasize it in the context of this brief discussion of longevity. One hears of lifelong harmonious marriages. Or productive marriages.

But how frequently does one hear of a lifelong passionate marriage? Newspapers frequently carry pictures of couples celebrating their fiftieth or sixtieth wedding anniversaries. Ponder these pictures. Time and again these long-married husbands and wives have a melancholy expression on their faces. They appear bored. In spite of this boredom husbands and wives—because of inertia and out of a sense of loyalty and indebtedness—remain in drab marriages. To seek a divorce would cause financial and emotional difficulties. And on top of all of that, some people might rationalize, it would "upset the grandkids." This spousal boredom explains why some husbands and wives inwardly (but with feelings of guilt) long for the death of their spouses. This spousal ennui partly explains why newspapers carry accounts of husbands murdering their wives and of wives murdering their husbands. I once attended a Methodist ministerial conference where a clergyman leading a discussion group asked the gathered ministers, "How many of you fellows have already picked out the woman you would ask to marry you if your wife died?" His question was answered with stunned silence. This spousal death desire is dealt with by Jane Shapiro in her novel *The Dangerous Husband*. Shapiro places on the lips of a wife this wish for her husband: "I wish his plane would crash."[12]

I am belaboring the insight that monogamy can produce monotony, which mutates marriage into a cradle of adultery. Wedlock becomes deadlock. In his novel *Too Far to Go*, John Updike observes that marriage is a "million mundane moments shared."[13] This marital monotony is explored in novels such as Tolstoy's *Anna Karenina*, Flaubert's *Madame Bovary*, Lawrence's *Lady Chatterly's Lover*, and Henry James's *The Golden Bowl*. In Flaubert's *Madame Bovary*, a French novel about infidelity, the heroine became unfaithful when life with her dull doctor husband became tedious and she found herself wondering if there was not more to life than her boring existence.

As an aside, how and why did Western societies end up with the veneration of monogamy? Tribal societies around the world—particularly in Africa—are polygamous. Islam permits multiple wives. Mohammed, Islam's founder, had thirteen wives. Osama bin Laden of

September 11th notoriety has four. Why Western societies are committed to monogamy is an anthropological puzzle. A common Western "solution" to monogamy is serial monogamy. People marry and divorce and then remarry and divorce and then remarry and divorce. This "solution" is pursued particularly by society's glitterati.

The conclusion of the matter: husbands and wives on occasion have extramarital affairs in order to escape the fatigue and boredom of lengthy marriages. This is what I mean by the longevity factor.

I shall now deal with a second factor that contributes to extramarital affairs: the biological desire or imperative (particularly on the part of men) for sexual variety. This factor can be labeled the "Jimmy Carter" factor. While a presidential candidate, Jimmy Carter, a man whom I admire, admitted in a controversial interview with *Playboy* magazine that on occasion he had committed "lust" in his heart. I interpret this confession to mean that on more than one occasion he had desired to copulate with a woman other than his wife. For making this admission he was denounced by conservative religious spokesmen. But I say: three cheers for Jimmy Carter! His admission brings into focus the insight that some people (both men and women) desire variety when it comes to sexual partners. This desire for variety is embedded in the Muslim belief that male martyrs—when they enter paradise—are given seventy-two beautiful female virgins with whom to have sex. This desire for variety is embedded in a remark made to me by an aristocratic lawyer's wife, "I wish I could have been a whore." The church—as well as Jimmy Carter—labels this desire for variety as lust. The person who thinks this way, traditional piety contends, has a "dirty mind." Consequently, the church and society urge people to suppress their desire for multifarious sexual encounters.

Yet protestations on the part of society and the church have not obliterated this desire for sexual variety. I do not see how anyone who has taken the time to read *The Myth of Monogamy* by David Barash and Judith Lipton can deny the reality and the potency of this desire, which is shared by some people. Years ago Dr. Alfred Kinsey in his book *Sexual Behavior in the Human Male* (a book denounced by Billy Graham) stated that

103

most males can immediately understand why most males want extramarital coitus. Although many of them refrain from engaging in such activity because they consider it morally unacceptable or socially undesirable, even such abstinent individuals can usually understand that sexual variety, new situations, and new partners might provide satisfactions which are no longer found in coitus which has been confined for some period of years to a single sexual partner. . . . On the other hand, many females find it difficult to understand why any male who is married should want to have coitus with any female other than his wife.[14]

This impulse toward sexual variety is reflected in the apocryphal story about President Coolidge and his wife. Legend has it that one day President and Mrs. Coolidge were visiting a government farm. Soon after their arrival they were taken off on separate tours. When Mrs. Coolidge passed the chicken pens she paused to ask the man in charge if the rooster copulated more than once each day. "Dozens of times" was the reply. "Please tell that to the president," Mrs. Coolidge requested. When the president passed the pens and was told about the rooster, he asked, "Same hen every time?" "Oh no, Mr. President, a different one each time." The president nodded slowly, then said, "Tell that to Mrs. Coolidge." Hence William James's ditty:

Higamous hogamous, a woman is monogamous.
Hogamous higamous, a man is polygamous.

Our fate as human beings is to live our lives within a complex network of biological inclinations, societal traditions, religious expectations, and personal experiences. Like it or not, marriages last longer than they once did. Consequently, these marriages can mutate into fatigued relationships. Like it or not, people—particularly men—are wired with a desire for multiple sexual partners. To deny this impulse would be as foolish as to deny the existence of the libido. Melt these two factors together (along with the fact that daily—on television, on the Internet, in publications—people are bombarded with multiple sexual stimuli) and I have no difficulty understanding why some men and women stray from the straight and narrow and engage in extramarital affairs.

Maybe what is needed is a reconceptualization of what marriage involves. Is it not the case that marriage suffers from what I have called an expectation overload? Does this expectation overload contribute to the current high divorce rate? Does it make sense to believe a man or a woman should live an entire life and receive sexual affection from only one person, namely, that person's husband or wife? Is the female demand for a romantic monopoly on husbands a manifestation of selfishness? Alas, I don't know the right answers to these questions. And alas, I doubt if a reconceptualization of marriage—particularly by the church—will happen in the foreseeable future.

I conclude with a plea for compassion. Relevant is the biblical episode where Jesus was confronted with a woman discovered in the act of adultery.

> Early in the morning he came again to the temple. All the people came to him and he sat down and began to teach them. The scribes and the Pharisees brought a woman who had been caught in adultery; and making her stand before all of them, they said to him, "Teacher, this woman was caught in the very act of committing adultery. Now in the law Moses commanded us to stone such women. Now what do you say?"
>
> They said this to test him, so that they might have some charge to bring against him. Jesus bent down and wrote with his finger on the ground. When they kept on questioning him, he straightened up and said to them, "Let anyone among you who is without sin be the first to throw a stone at her." And once again he bent down and wrote on the ground. When they heard it, they went away, one by one, beginning with the elders; and Jesus was left alone with the woman standing before him. Jesus straightened up and said to her, "Woman, where are they? Has no one condemned you?" She said, "No one, sir." And Jesus said, "Neither do I condemn you. Go your way, and from now on do not sin again." (John 8:2–11)

Notice Jesus' words: "Let anyone among you who is without sin be the first to throw a stone at her"; "Neither do I condemn you." I suggest that the church today would do well to imitate Jesus' attitude and behavior the day he found himself confronting a person who was an adulteress. To wit: more compassion and less condemnation.

NOTES

1. Rabbi Jeffrey Howard Tigay, "Adultery," *Encyclopedia Judaica* (New York: Macmillan, 1971), 314.

2. *Catechism of the Catholic Church* (Liguori, Mo.: Liguori Publications, 1994), 572, paragraph 2380.

3. Ibid., 565, paragraph 2353.

4. William Edward Hartpole Lecky, *A History of European Morals from Augustus to Charlemagne* (New York: Arno Press, 1975), 2: 122.

5. Bertrand Russell, *Marriage and Morals* (New York: Liveright Publishing Corporation, 1929), 49.

6. Lecky, *European Morals*, 108.

7. John Witte Jr., *From Sacrament to Contract* (Louisville, Ky.: Westminster John Knox Press, 1977), 23.

8. Ibid.

9. David Olson and John DeFrain, *Marriages and Family* (New York: McGraw Hill, 2006), 9.

10. This account of the Harris tragedy is based on articles by Ruth Rendon, which appeared in the July 22, 2002, and the January 19, 2003, editions of the *Houston Chronicle*. Clara Harris is now serving a twenty-year prison sentence for murdering her husband.

11. Stephanie Coontz, *The Way We Never Were* (New York: Basic Books, 1992).

12. Jane Shapiro, *The Dangerous Husband* (New York: Little, Brown, 1999), 126.

13. John Updike, *Too Far to Go* (New York: Fawcett Crest, 1979), 10.

14. This Kinsey quotation appears without source or page citation in David Barash and Judith Lipton, *The Myth of Monogamy* (New York: W. H. Freeman & Company, 2001), 21.

CHAPTER 6

Prostitution and
the Harm Principle

Finally, I shall deal briefly with prostitution. To my mind prostitution (indulging in sexual acts with another person in return for a fee) is aesthetically repulsive. I could not endure the thought of either my daughter or granddaughter becoming prostitutes. For either of them to become harlots would break my heart.

Yet prostitution, practiced by males and females, has been around for a long time. Referred to as the world's oldest profession, prostitution is evidenced throughout human history. Reference has previously been made in this book to the Gilgamesh Epic, the oldest known epic in Western civilization, which was discovered back in the nineteenth century in the library of Ashurbanipal, the last strong ruler of the Assyrian city of Nineveh. One of the characters in this literary work has the strange name of Enkidu and is a wild forest creature. The Gilgamesh Epic relates that an attempt was made to humanize Enkidu by having him copulate with a prostitute.[1]

In addition, the Old Testament reveals that prostitutes were a part of Jewish society. Genesis, the first book in the Bible, tells of Tamar's transitory harlotry with her father-in-law (Gen 38:12–26). Joshua's

spies, sent out to reconnoiter the promised land, spent time in the house
of Rahab the harlot (Josh 2). Picaresque Samson patronized a harlot at
Gaza (Judg 16). King Solomon, known for his wisdom, settled a dispute
between two harlots (1 Kgs 3:16–28). Harlots practiced their trade in
Solomon's Temple (2 Kgs 23:7), played the harp and sang songs (Isa
23:16), and bathed in the pool of Samaria (1 Kgs 22:38). In none of
these episodes (except 2 Kgs 23:7) is harlotry condemned. Incidentally,
houses of prostitution exist today in the modern state of Israel. These
bordellos are patronized by Orthodox rabbis among others.

In the ancient Near East, sacred prostitution (*hierodouleia*) was
widely practiced and involved male or female prostitutes. In the temples of Ishtar, Astarte (mentioned in the Bible as the female consort of
Baal), and Aphrodite, women offered themselves sexually to strangers.
Evidently the belief existed that by copulating with temple prostitutes a
person was communicating with the gods. References to these female
prostitutes appear on the Law Code of Hammurabi, a stone inscription
that is one of the earliest legal texts from the ancient Near East.[2] Furthermore, Herodotus, the father of history, reported that in ancient
Babylon women were required to attend the temple of Ishtar at least
once during their lifetimes in order to have intercourse with strangers.[3]
According to the Old Testament, cult prostitution involving male prostitutes was practiced by the Jews (1 Kgs 14:24; 2 Kgs 23:7).

Early Greek society had aristocratic prostitutes. They were known
as the *hetaerae*. The Athenian orator Demosthenes described a tripar-
tite division of women in Greek society as follows: "The *hetaerae* we
keep for the sake of pleasure; concubines are for the daily care of our
persons, but wives to bear us legitimate children and to be faithful
guardians of our households."[4]

Prostitution has been a part of American society from colonial days
to the present. Benjamin Franklin, the sage of Philadelphia and an active
participant in the Constitutional Convention, wrote a work entitled
Advice to a Young Man on the Choice of a Mistress. Franklin listed eight
reasons why young men should prefer older mistresses.

- Older women have greater knowledge of the world.

- "When women cease to be handsome, they study to be good. To maintain their influence over men, they supply the diminution of beauty by an augmentation of utility."

- There is no hazard of children.

- They are more discreet in conducting an affair.

- Although an older woman could be distinguished from a younger one by her face, "regarding only what is below the girdle, it is impossible of two women to know an old from a young one."

- Because "the sin is less. The debauching of a virgin may be her ruin, and make her for life unhappy."

- Likewise, "the compunction is less. The having made a young girl *miserable* may give you frequent bitter reflections; none of which can attend the making an old woman *happy*."

- Finally, older women are to be preferred because "they are *so grateful!*"[5]

Forms of prostitution differ. One form: mistress keeping. Another form: streetwalking, that is, prostitutes openly soliciting clients from among the people walking city streets. Still another form: bar girls who entertain male customers in bars and nightclubs, encourage them to spend money, and make themselves available for copulation at a price. Yet another form: call girls who work out of private quarters, often with a repertoire of regular customers. A newer form of prostitution involves "massage parlors," which time and again are de facto bordellos. And then there are prostitutes who ply their trade in brothels (like the brothels in Nevada). This prostitution subculture has a lingo all its own. For example, a hos (a contraction of "whore" that rhymes with "rose") is a streetwalker. Prostitutes are known as hustlers and hookers. A pimp is a male who secures customers for prostitutes. A john (a term used contemptuously) is a customer of a prostitute. What point am I making? Prostitution, openly practiced in European cities such as Rotterdam, has been around for a long, long time, having multiple forms, having its own language.

Maybe there is a sliver of truth in the poignant remark that prostitutes are human sacrifices that society offers on the altar of monogamy. And maybe there is a sliver of truth in the widely quoted medieval contention that prostitutes are like "sewers in the palace. Take away the sewers and you will fill the palace with pollution."[6]

Any person tempted to think a prostitute's life is glamorous should read Polly Adler's autobiography *A House Is Not a Home*. The author, born in Russia in the village of Yanow close to the Polish border, was the daughter of a Jewish tailor. While a young girl she emigrated to America and eventually became a madam in a brothel. For twenty-five years Adler operated New York City's most famous bordello. Her bordello, which she closed in 1945, reached the zenith of its fame during the Roaring Twenties. With reference to prostitutes in general, Polly Adler wrote:

> By becoming a prostitute, a girl cuts herself off not merely from her family, but from such a great part of life. She is isolated not just by social custom but by working conditions, and she has to some extent deprived herself of her rights as a citizen for she has forfeited the protection of the law. It is not syphilis which is the occupational disease of the prostitute, but loneliness. And no one yet has discovered a miracle drug to cure it.[7]

Adler went ahead to observe that for ninety-nine out of a hundred prostitutes

> going to bed with a customer is a joyless, even distasteful, experience. No girl, as a social worker once said, sets out to be a prostitute. Such stupidity would be incredible. Who wants to be a pariah, a social outcast—treated with contempt, jailed, beaten, robbed and finally kicked into the gutter when she is no longer salable? A prostitute can count on no more than ten money-making years. Then she is through—if not dead or diseased, so broken by drugs, alcohol and the steady abuse of her body that no one will hire her again. And since the sordid and

pitiful fate of the prostitute is far from being a secret, no wonder people ask what propels a girl into this short and unhappy life.

No doubt there are as many answers to this question as there are sociologists, psychiatrists, philosophers and doctors of divinity. But in my opinion the greatest single factor—and the common denominator in an overwhelming majority of cases—is poverty. It is true that, though many girls are poor, only a small percentage of them take to hustling. But there is more than one kind of poverty—there is emotional poverty and intellectual poverty and poverty of spirit. As well as material lacks, there can be a lack of love, a lack of education, a lack of hope. And out of such impoverishment the prostitute is bred. (127–28)

In view of Adler's remarks about the sad and sordid life of prostitutes, does prostitution pass what I have called the harm test? Some persons may want to argue: "If a customer and a prostitute copulate, what harm have they done? None." But this line of reasoning is fallacious because it fails to take into account the harm that—over time—prostitution does to the prostitute. Prostitution, alas, is an entrenched tragedy.

Curiously and unexpectedly, in her autobiography Polly Adler offered shrewd advice for wives of men who patronize bordellos. She labels some wives as being "whores in everything but name."

I truly do believe that nine times out of ten a wife could keep her husband on the reservation if she used half the effort to hold him that she did to hook him. When a woman sets her cap for a guy, she goes all out to be attractive to him. She keeps herself groomed to perfection, she always has that dab of perfume in the right place, she laughs at his jokes, she goes along with his whims, she flirts with other men just enough to keep him up on the bit, and whatever she does, she convinces him she does it all for great big wonderful Him. But after girl gets boy, why should a two-buck marriage license entitle her to turn off all that charm she turned on during the courtship? Why doesn't she continue to dress up for him? Why doesn't she use her eyes to see how he's feeling, and her ears to listen to him, and her tongue for compliments and interesting conversation instead of digs and gossip about her neighbors? And why, after waving her sex like a flag to get him, doesn't she at least pretend to enjoy his caresses? And yet I suppose I should thank such wives instead of criticizing them—they helped keep me in business.

Why wouldn't a man turn from such a wife to my girls, who were always beautifully groomed and lovely to look at and gay and responsive, who were always flattering him, sympathizing with him, telling him what a terrific lover he was? Of course they were getting paid for it, but doesn't a wife get paid too? It is not a new point of view, but so far as I'm concerned a prostitute is anyone who sells herself for gain. The women who take husbands not out of love but out of greed, to get their bills paid, to get a fine house and clothes and jewels; the women who marry to get out of a tiresome job, or to get away from disagreeable relatives, or to avoid being called an old maid—these are whores in everything but name. The only difference between them and my girls is that my girls gave a man his money's worth. (226–37)

The late Alfred Kinsey of Indiana University wrote in a vein similar to Polly Adler, the bordello madam:

Most of the male's extra-marital activity is undoubtedly a product of his interest in a variety of experience. On the other hand, there is certainly a portion of his extra-marital intercourse which is the product of unsatisfactory relations with his wife. When she fails to be interested in sexual relations with her husband, when she is less interested than he is, when she refuses to allow the variety in pre-coital techniques that the male would like to have, or when she accedes to such techniques without evidencing an interest equal to that of the male, she is encouraging him to find extra-marital relations. The wife's refusal of mouth-genital contacts with her husband is a factor in sending some males elsewhere for such experience.[8]

To make a long story short: prostitution is here to stay. A societal universal, prostitution is found around the world: in Europe, in Asia, in North and South America, and in sub-Saharan Africa. Several of my university colleagues traveled recently through sub-Saharan Africa (visiting countries such as Nigeria). On returning from this African tour one of them remarked to me, "At night we had to fight off the whores." In the East, Japan has developed the institution of the geisha, a sophisticated entertainer similar to the Greek *hetaerae*. Geishas include sexual intercourse in their repertoire of services. Indeed, prostitution is more prevalent in Southeast Asia, where it is a parasite on the region's poverty, than any other place on earth, Prostitution is the only way some women in this part of the world keep body and soul together. Today Bangkok in Thailand and Manila in the Philippines are centers of an international tourist-sex industry.

In the Western world valiant attempts have been made to repress prostitution. These repressive countermeasures have not been successful. The reason for their lack of success is economic. Prostitution offers at a cost customers are willing to pay an activity (transitory and emotionally uninvolved sexual encounters) for which there is an unending demand. Prostitutes want the money; their clients crave the sexual experience.

Society and the church face two alternatives in regard to prostitution. The first alternative is to continue the policy of viewing prostitution as an illegal, criminal activity. For prostitutes this alternative presents all kinds of problems and dangers: prurient harassment by the police, exploitation by pimps, exposure to venereal diseases, and brutalization by customers. These problems and dangers are experienced particularly by streetwalkers. Time and again newspapers carry accounts of streetwalkers being murdered by their clients. I can think of few sights more pathetic than the spectacle of a streetwalker in Atlanta or Los Angeles with heavy makeup on her face, dressed in skimpy, provocative clothes, walking in high-heeled shoes, and forced to listen to passersby who callously bombard her with derisive insults: "Hey, sweetheart! You're a slut! Ain't you."

The second alternative is to decriminalize prostitution and bring it under government regulation (as the state of Nevada has done). Across the years, as I previously observed, prostitution has persevered in spite of sustained efforts by law enforcement officials to eradicate it. So why not be realistic? Make prostitution legal and bring it under government regulation. For our country to decriminalize prostitution would not be without precedent. Most European countries do not consider prostitution a criminal offense. Indeed—as Ellen Pillard of the University of Nevada in Reno—has observed: "The United States is the only industrialized country that in large measure continues to criminalize prostitution."

113

Arguments for decriminalization and governmental regulation are multiple. The strongest argument for regulated prostitution is that—from the standpoint of health—it is safer than illegal sex. Prostitutes would be required to have frequent tests for venereal diseases. Decriminalization would end the humiliating system in which prostitutes are arrested by policemen, jailed and fined, and then released to go back to work. Regulation would reduce the brutalization of prostitutes. And it would reduce the possibility of police bribery. Legalized prostitution could be a source of tax revenue. Solon, the Athenian lawgiver, filled brothels with female slaves, taxed their income, and used part of this income to build a temple to Aphrodite, the goddess of love.

Opponents of decriminalization must remember that decriminalization does not mean moral approval. I am old enough to remember when states in the Deep South did not allow liquor sales. Prohibition was the order of the day. States were "dry" and Will Rogers quipped, "The South is dry and will vote dry. That is everybody that is sober enough to stagger to the polls."[9] Bootlegging and crime flourished. A happier state of affairs now exists with southern states controlling the sale of intoxicating beverages. State control has resulted in less crime and less public drunkenness. But state control does not mean the state approves of people consuming alcoholic beverages. Similarly, state control of prostitution would not mean the state approves of prostitution.

Is there any possibility of prostitution being decriminalized in the United States in the near future? The answer: No! Such a proposal would bring down the wrath of the church and the wrath of conservative politicians. But people's opinions change with the passing of time. Maybe decriminalization and state control will be a possibility a hundred years from now. But not now.

NOTES

1. The sexual relationship between Enkidu and a harlot is dealt with on pages 62 through 69 in *The Epic of Gilgamesh*. The epic relates that Enkidu and the harlot lay together for six days and seven nights at the end of which Enkidu

was sexually satisfied. N. K. Sanders, trans., *The Epic of Gilgamesh* (London: Penguin Books, 1972), 65.

2. *Law Code of Hammurabi* found on pp. 163 through 177 of James Pritchard, ed., *Ancient Near Eastern Texts* (Princeton: Princeton University Press, 1955). Paragraph 181 on page 174 refers to a father who dedicates his daughter to a deity in order for her to become a sacred prostitute.

3. Book 1, paragraph 199 on page 251 of *Herodotus* (Cambridge: Harvard University Press, 1966). Quoted in *History of Herodotus* in the Loeb Classical Library published by Harvard University Press.

4. Quoted in Paul Abramson and Steven Pinkerton, *With Pleasure* (Oxford: Oxford University Press, 2002), 76.

5. Ibid., 198.

6. This sewer metaphor is traditionally ascribed to Augustine of Hippo and to Thomas Aquinas. For example, see page 254 of the thirteenth-century work entitled *De Regimine Principum* by Ptolemy of Lucca (Philadelphia: University of Pennsylvania Press, 1997), translated by James M. Blythe. Scholars like Istvan Bejczy contend, however, the metaphor's ascription to Augustine and Aquinas is a mistake. See page 373 of Bejczy's article entitled "Tolerantia: a Medieval Concept" on pages 365 to 384 of the *Journal of the History of Ideas* 58.3 (1997). Although they did not use the sewer metaphor, both Augustine and Aquinas made it clear they viewed prostitution as a necessary evil.

7. Polly Adler, *A House Is Not a Home* (New York: Rinehart & Company, 1953), 125.

8. Alfred C. Kinsey, Wardell B. Pomeroy, and Clyde E. Martin, *Sexual Behavior in the Human Male* (Philadelphia: W. B. Saunders Company, 1948), 590.

9. Will Rogers, *The Autobiography of Will Rogers* (Boston: Houghton Mifflin, 1926), 141.

CHAPTER 7

Some Concluding Remarks

As far as human sexuality is concerned, the church time and again has fumbled the ball. One obvious fumble: the church's creation of shame language. Across the centuries the church has gone out of its way to infuse shame into the words people use to denote sexual behavior. A husband who engages in extramarital sex is said to be cheating on his wife. Who can use such words as original sin, concupiscence, adultery, fornication, masturbation, sodomy, and onanism without sensing the stigma of Christian shaming? No wonder Christians experience remorse while engaging in sex; the language they use codes shame into their sexual activities. And no wonder Christians condemn themselves for their sexual longings.

The church has also fumbled the ball by creating Procrustean rules for sexual behavior. Procrustes in Greek legend was a giant robber who lived in Eleusis, a city some thirteen miles northwest of Athens. He lured travelers to his house under the pretense that he was going to entertain them. Instead of entertaining them, he forced travelers to lie down on an iron bed. If they were taller or shorter than this iron bed, Procrustes chopped off or stretched their limbs accordingly. He was eventually slain by Theseus, an Athenian king. The term Procrustean has come to signify the use of arbitrary and coercive methods; unfortunately, Procrustean rules and methods abound in church teachings about human sexuality. To wit: "Celibacy is superior to marriage." From the beginning the Christian movement was obsessed with celibacy. Saint Paul wished that all disciples were unmarried like him (1 Cor 7:1, 7). The Revelation to John has a reference to the 144,000 saints who "made it" to heaven (Rev 14:1). They are described as those "who have not defiled themselves with women for they are virgins" (Rev 14:4).

Other Procrustean teachings involve masturbation, homosexuality, and a host of other sexual behaviors: "Masturbation is wrong"; "Both premarital and extramarital sex are sinful"; "Homosexual liaisons are an abomination"; "Sexual intercourse between unmarried persons is immoral"; "Concupiscence—the spontaneous arousal of the libido—is adultery." The way members of the clergy thunder these rules from pulpits would lead one to think they were handed down from on high at Mount Sinai. Tragically, the church advocates these Procrustean rules without a trace of compassion and without bothering to engage in casuistry: moral reasoning to explain *why* a given activity is wrong. The church's draconian attitude toward human sexuality explains—at least in part—why some Christians have decided to join the church alumni association.

A military maxim affirms: A wise general knows not only how to advance but also how to retreat. Maybe the moment has arrived when the church should throw in the towel and get completely out of the "sex advice" business. If that is an impossibility, I suggest that the moment has arrived when the church needs to retreat from severe positions taken on human sexuality. In Greek mythology Eros was the god of love; in English the term eros has come to mean erotic love or desire. Going back particularly to theologians such as Augustine, the church has submerged eros in a marinade of shame, sinfulness, and guilt. Truth resides in Friedrich Nietzsche's remark: "Christianity gave Eros poison to drink. He didn't die from it, but he did degenerate into a vice."[1] Instead of viewing eros as vice, the church should view eros as sacred—a gift from God. Such a revision would lead the church to abandon its irrational devotion to celibacy. Such a revision would also lead the church to abandon its view that the only valid setting for the erotic is marriage.

Are such revisions possible? Candidly, I don't know. Only the future will tell. But one or two things I do know. First, the church has its troubles. The church has been abandoned by this country's glitterati, the beautiful and sophisticated people one reads about in *Time, Newsweek,* and the *New York Times.* The church has been abandoned by this country's intelligentsia. How many Sunday School classes for young people are taught by university physics professors? And the church has been abandoned by this country's corporate leaders. How many church activities are sponsored week after week by presidents of major corporations listed on the New York Stock Exchange? In the face of these abandonments the church—like a fish out of water—poignantly flops around seeking to become relevant. The announcements that appear on "church news pages" in newspapers (usually in Saturday editions) reflect this flopping. A reading of these pages reveals the following kinds of church activities: priestly blessings—complete with the sprinkling of holy water—on members of local motorcycle clubs as well as on their motorcycles; hat parades for senior ladies; Valentine's Day parties; patriotic celebrations (with fireworks) on the Fourth of July; healthy-emphasis weekends featuring discussions of vegetarian cooking and natural remedies for colds and sore throats; computer classes for the computer illiterate; cooking schools for new brides; gardening classes for retired citizens; seminars for divorced people; premarital counseling sessions for brides and grooms; pizza and television parties for teenagers; and Halloween hayrides for young folks. Best of all: dedicatory services for family pets. What this whirligig of activities has to do with Jesus, the crucified Jew, is not obvious.

Second, the moment has arrived when the church would benefit from an aggressive anticlericalism. By anticlericalism I mean a movement (composed of lay persons) that evaluates, critiques, and challenges the clergy concerning their beliefs and practices. Embodying at times attitudes of skepticism and resentment, anticlericalism has the capacity

119

to question the extravagant influence exerted by the clergy on occasion with regard to moral, religious, and political issues. The clergy can exert this influence because increasingly Christianity is becoming a middle-class (bourgeois) movement composed of people who don't think for themselves. Parenthetically, anticlericalism is not a new idea; it has been around for a long time. It erupted in the Middle Ages as a by-product of the conflict between the papacy and secular authorities. This medieval conflict came to a boil in the year 1077 at Canossa in the struggle between Pope Gregory VII (Hildebrand) and the German emperor Henry IV. Anticlericalism was also a potent element in the Reformation when Protestants emphasized the priesthood of all believers and deem-phasized the role of ordained clerics. During the Enlightenment anti-clericalism flourished in Europe—particularly in countries in which the Roman Catholic Church was prominent. Anticlericalism was particu-larly intense in France.

Anticlericalism has never played a prominent role on the American ecclesiastical scene. I suggest, however, that a generous dose of anticler-icalism would do the American church a lot of good. For decades the clergy (never debating with critics, never being called on the carpet) has considered itself above criticism and has gotten away with being moral bullies. Members of the clergy need to be challenged because some of them are purveyors of ignorance, of disinformation. With a sad heart I have witnessed members of the clergy spreading disinformation. My fate was to be born in the Deep South and to be socialized into the Southern Baptist denomination (of which I am no longer a member). In the 1950s I spent eight years beyond college earning two theological degrees from the Southern Baptist Theological Seminary in Louisville, Kentucky. At that time Southern Seminary's faculty was superb. They immersed our minds in post-Enlightenment biblical scholarship. As a seminarian I had no way of foreseeing the transformation the denomi-nation would undergo during the closing decades of the twentieth cen-tury. The denomination was taken over hook, line, and sinker by biblical fundamentalists—people who insist that the Bible is an inerrant, infallible document. To be sure, the Bible is one of the world's most influential and significant books. But alas! It is not inerrant or infallible. The Bible has a human side. It contains mistaken scientific ideas and historical contradictions and it advocates practices (such as genocide and slavery) that are morally untenable. I watched the fundamentalist takeover of my denomination with dismay and then with despair. This takeover could have been avoided if the Baptist laity had seen fit to study the issues and to challenge fire-eating fundamentalist preachers to defend their views. But instead of becoming involved, the majority chose to sit on their hands and do nothing. As one layman remarked to me, "The whole controversy is nothing but a preacher's fight." Today the Southern Baptist denomination is a Jerry Falwell fortress and has become the laughingstock of American Protestantism. Consequently, I will go down to my grave burdened with melancholy and with a sense of betrayal. And I will go down to my grave knowing that the denomination I once loved so deeply is propagating a message that is intellectually dishonest. All of this could have been avoided if a vigorous anticlericalism had been on the scene.

What about a need for anticlericalism in the Roman Catholic Church? A study of the church's official 1994 catechism reveals that its authors are blissfully ignorant of contemporary biblical scholarship. A study of this catechism also reveals that the Catholic Church holds beliefs that are grotesque. Does any rational person believe that the stigma of original sin (going back to Adam and Eve in the garden of Eden) has been passed on for thousands of years from one generation to the next through semen? An aggressive anticlericalism would call such a grotesque belief into question. Indeed, the contemporary Catholic Church needs to reevaluate its beliefs. Are they credible? Or have some suffered a depletion of plausibility?

The church has done a superb job in the area of textual evaluation (criticism) of the Bible. Were verses 9–19 originally a part of the sixteenth chapter of Mark's gospel? Were verses 1–11 originally a part of the eighth chapter of John's gospel? The church has also done a superb job in the area of literary evaluation (criticism) of the Bible. Was the sixteenth chapter an original part of Paul's letter to the Roman Christians? Does 2 Corinthians consist of fragments of several letters written by Saint Paul? I agree with John Bowden, author of *Jesus: The Unanswered Questions*, that the time has now arrived when the church should engage in belief or doctrinal evaluation (criticism). Does it make sense for the church to continue proclaiming that Jesus is infallible? Does it make sense for the church to continue believing that Christianity is the only valid religion? If the church is not concerned with the authenticity—the integrity—of what it teaches, it runs the risk of becoming an ideological house of cards.

Moreover, I suggest that a vigorous anticlericalism is needed both within Roman Catholicism and Protestantism because many church members do not understand that the clergy can be an instrument of the demonic. They have never pondered Christopher Marlowe's play entitled *Dr. Faustus*. At one point in this sixteenth-century drama, Dr. Faustus is confronted by a repulsive-looking devil named Mephistopheles. Responding to Mephistopheles' ugly body and face, Dr. Faustus proposes that this devil go away and then reappear to him in an attractive form:

I charge thee to return and change thy shape;
Thou art too ugly to attend on me.
Go, and return an old Franciscan friar;
That holy shape becomes a devil best.[2]

Ponder the words: the holy shape of a Franciscan friar is the shape that best becomes a devil. Pursuing Faustus's request, Mephistopheles goes away and reappears as an elderly Franciscan friar—a priest who is a vehicle of the demonic. The clergy serving as vehicles of the demonic is tragically a factor on the contemporary religious scene. Persons who are ordained, have earned theological degrees, wear ecclesiastical garb, and participate in worship services (doing everything from confessing the Apostles' Creed to swinging incense pots) can be personifications of evil. They can be among the meanest people on earth (an insight it took me a lifetime to acquire). Consider fire-breathing fundamentalists who drive "liberals" out of the church because they do not accept every wrinkle of orthodox theology. Consider pedophile priests who sexually abuse altar boys. I shall never forget a lecture I heard in Atlanta at the 2003 meeting of the American Academy of Religion. The lecture was given by a man who—when he was an altar boy—was sexually abused by a Roman Catholic priest. In his lecture he related how as a youngster he stood in awe of priests, who had—so he had been taught—the power to transform wine into the blood of Jesus. Being in awe of one who possessed such power, the lecturer related how he did not have the will to resist a priest who engaged him repeatedly in fellatio. For generations priests have gotten away with such behavior. They have been able to do so because the laity either didn't care or thought the clergy were "too sacred" to be criticized, questioned, and held accountable. Any Catholic Christian devoted to celibacy—a contributing factor to pedophilia—should be required to read A. W. Richard Sipe's book entitled *Celibacy in Crisis*, which I mentioned earlier in chapter 3. As the title suggests, this book is a critique of celibacy. Its foreword, by Richard McBrien of Notre Dame University, observes that

> obligatory celibacy and the church's official teaching on human sexuality are at the root of the worst crisis the Catholic Church has faced since the time of the Reformation. The Church's teaching (on human sexuality) is that every sexual thought, word, desire, and action outside of marriage (and some within), as, for example, the use of contraception, are gravely sinful and deserving of eternal punishment in Hell if the sin is not properly confessed and absolved before death.

I am suggesting that only a lay anticlericalism can grapple with and change such a benighted view. I contend that this anticlericalism must be a lay movement—completely independent of the church. Lay involvement is the only means by which Mephistophelian members of the clergy can be exposed, questioned, and cut down to size. Moreover, lay involvement is crucial because lay influence is a potent force that keeps the clergy within the bounds of common sense.

NOTES

1. Friedrich Nietzsche, *Jenseits von Gut and Böse* (Beyond Good and Evil), no. 168, in Giorgio Colli and Mazzino Montinari, ed., *Sämtliche Werke: Kritische Studienausgabe*, 2nd ed. (New York: de Gruyter, 1988), 5:102.

2. Act 1, scene iii, lines 22–25 in *Doctor Faustus* by Christopher Marlowe. See Irving Ribner, ed., *The Complete Works of Christopher Marlowe* (New York: Odyssey Press, 1963), 364–65.

INDEX